YOU'RE NOT FOOLING ANYONE WHEN YOU TAKE YOUR LAPTOP TO A COFFEE SHOP:

Scalzi on Writing

YOU'RE NOT FOOLING ANYONE WHEN YOU TAKE YOUR LAPTOP TO A COFFEE SHOP:

Scalzi on Writing

John Scalzi

Subterranean Press ✦ 2007

You're Not Fooling Anyone When You Take Your
Laptop to a Coffee Shop: Scalzi on Writing

Copyright © 2007 by John Scalzi.
All rights reserved.

Second Printing

ISBN
978-1-59606-063-0

Subterranean Press
PO Box 190106
Burton, MI 48519

www.subterraneanpress.com

～ Table of Contents ～

Chapter 3: The Schadenfreude Needle
is Buried Deep into the Red: On Writers 189

INTRODUCTIONS
~~||||~~ AND ~~||||~~
CAVEAT EMPTORS

H i there.

This is a book about writing. But! It is not a book about *how* to write. God knows there are enough books on that particular subject, not to mention classes and workshops and Web sites and public television shows, and the thought of trying to cram another one of those books down the gullet of the public makes me want to jam my head into the nearest garbage disposal. I barely know how *I* write; trying to tell others how *they* should write seems fraught with peril. My only real advice to you in that regard is to find a nice, strenuous composition class so you don't get tripped up by the laughable mess that is English language grammar, and then write and write and write and write, and then write some more. That's what worked for me, so far as I can tell.

So there: if you were looking for my advice on how to write, you're done! That was easy. Set this book down and go about your life. I look forward to reading your books.

This is about everything *else* to do with writing, from the business of writing, to the stupid things writers do to sabotage themselves, to how writers interact with other writers, to various thoughts about the different sorts of writing out there. In short, it's about the writing *life*—or at the very least, *my* writing life, which is the one I am most qualified to discuss.

The essays you'll read in this book are entries that I have written over a five year period (from 2001 to early 2006) on my personal Web site, the Whatever (http://scalzi.com/whatever). During this time I've written and/or published and/or signed contracts for ten books, wrote for newspapers and magazines, was paid to blog and write online, and wrote lots of anonymous but stupidly lucrative corporate work. It's been an interesting time in my writing life, and through all of it I've been posting my thoughts about writing (and *my* writing) online.

Since these entries are tied in to my professional writing life to a greater or lesser extent, they tend to be practical-minded; not so much about the *art* of writing as the *practice* of it. As I say a number of places in the book, I love writing but I'm not especially romantic about it. It's groovy to talk about writing as this great *thing*, but my mortgage is due at the first of the month, and paying that is a great thing, too. This is off-putting to some folks; I totally understand that. This probably won't be your kind of book if these practical aspects of the writing life don't hold much interest to you.

On the other hand, if you *are* interested in what it's like to be a full-time working writer here in the first slice of the twenty-first century, I think there'll be a lot for you here. I don't know about anyone else who writes for a living, but I've been having a hell of a lot of *fun* these last few years doing this job. It's a good and exciting time to be a writer, and I think that comes through. At the very least, I guarantee you that if I have managed to transmit half of what being a writer is like these days, you won't be bored reading this.

This book is organized very loosely into four chapters. The first chapter is actual writing advice, because even though this isn't a book on how to write, if you *are* writing, there's lots to say about it. The second chapter is about the writing life—I write a lot about money there. The third chapter is on writers, and mostly about writers doing stupid things. Think of this chapter largely as cautionary tales. The final chapter is about science fiction, the genre in which I wrote almost all of my fiction so far. Read it even if you don't read science fiction; a lot of what's written about there is applicable across genres.

The entries in these chapters skip back and forth across time—they're arranged mostly for flow and for interest. Lots of topics will get explored but I suspect some topics will not always be explored to everyone's satisfaction—there's only so much space and so many things to cover. But I write at the Whatever on a close to daily basis—if there's something about writing you'd like to ask me, you can always drop me an e-mail (john@scalzi.com) and maybe I'll write about it there. If I get enough questions, maybe I'll be able to crank out a sequel to this in 2010. Everyone wins.

I hope you enjoy the book. Thanks for reading.

— John Scalzi
January 24, 2006.

Dedicated to Laurence McMillin,
who is not here to know;

And to Daniel Mainz, who is.

WRITING ADVICE,
OR,
AVOIDING REAL WORK
THE JOHN SCALZI WAY

I had the "I'm gonna be a writer" epiphany when I was in my first year in high school, and realized something important, which was that for me writing was easy while everything else was actual work. Someone else with more personal fortitude might have brushed aside his or her limitations and done something else with their life, but as for me I followed the path of least resistance and became a writer. Because, man, I've seen other people do real work, and I have to say: real work sucks.

But now, 15 years into the whole "writing career" thing, I'm here to tell you that I was cruelly deceived by my own attempts at sloth: Turns out writing—if you actually want to make a living from it, and I do—really *is* actual work. Naturally when I discovered this I was appalled and dismayed, but since at the time I was too far into the writing hole to be qualified to do any other sort of work that didn't involve a price check or reading a telemarketing script (which is even *more* like real work than what I was doing), I had no choice but to continue .

Fortunately, overall things have turned out pretty well for me so far with this writing thing I've got going. By the end of 2006 I'll have published eleven books, fiction and non-fiction both, and aside from that I'll have written just about every sort of commercial writing there is to write save for a movie script (that's a special sort of hellish endeavor I suspect I would need to start drinking in order to contemplate). So, if you're looking for advice on how to break into Hollywood: Sorry. Check with Robert McKee. I hear he's good.

But as for the *rest* of it, here are my thoughts, in advice-like form—indeed, much of this chapter takes the form of numbered lists and bullet points, which is your assurance of quality advice. I suppose I could have gone whole hog and made this entire chapter a Powerpoint presentation. But then someone would have had to kill me. Besides, I'll save that for my series of lectures on writing at the Learning Annex. You'll come, won't you?

Actually, here's a disclaimer that you won't get from the writing guy down at the Learning Annex: With this advice, your mileage may vary (I repeat this little tidbit in the entries themselves). There are in fact many, many ways to have a happy and successful writing career. This is how I did it and what I recommend others do. Some of it may work for you. Some of it may not. You're a smart person; you know what's going on in your life and your career. Take the stuff that's useful for you and use it. Kick the rest to the curb.

Here we go.

JOHN SCALZI'S UTTERLY USELESS WRITING ADVICE

(October 2001, and updated since)

P eople are always asking me for advice on how to become a writer, because they assume (ha!) that I am a successful writer. My psychological and egotistical needs being what they are, I won't argue this point. I am, in fact, a fairly successful writer, if you define success as "making a good living doing nothing but writing." I do make a good living; I don't do anything else for a living but write. (If you define success as "being Stephen King," of course, I'm a miserable freakin' failure. But let's not.)

I've been a professional writer since June of 1990, when I got my first paid writing job as an intern for the *San Diego Tribune*, where I wrote music and concert reviews and other entertainment pieces. That was the summer before my senior year in college; when I got back to college, I wrote freelance entertainment articles for the *Chicago Sun-Times*. After college, I got—far more through an amazing stroke of luck and the fact that I was dirt cheap than by my own talents, let's be clear—a job as the movie critic for the *Fresno Bee*. I did that for five years, after which I joined AOL as its on-staff writer and editor. AOL laid me off in 1998 (this is a polite way of saying I was fired, since it was a layoff of one) and I became a freelance writer. I've been doing this ever since.

Being a freelance writer is interesting and not really a good thing for people who don't enjoy a permanent sense of panic. Be that as it may, it's done very well for me both financially (as a freelancer I make a healthy multiple of what I ever made working full-time for anyone) and career-wise, since I now write fluently on quite a number of subjects, including entertainment, humor, personal finance, online media, science, politics and even food and gardening.

I write for online clients and for offline clients. I consult with marketing companies on writing and creative issues, and have worked on marketing campaigns for very large corporations and financial institutions you've definitely heard of. I've had several books published, contributed to others and have more in the pipeline, and I look forward to writing books off and on for the rest of my professional life.

In short, I've reached a point in my career where I do feel confident about my ability to make a living writing, and I feel confident sharing some of my thoughts and experiences on the matter.

So. What follows is exactly that: my thoughts on the writing life—largely from the freelance writing perspective—and how to live it. Bear in mind that these comments are based solely on my own thoughts and experiences and may not jibe with anything else you've heard anywhere from anyone else. Also bear in mind that I may be completely full of crap. On the other hand, and I say this as dispassionately as possible, I make a buttload of money doing what I do, so I must be doing *something* right. If you can figure out what it is, please be sure to tell me.

(So how much do I actually make? I'm not going to give a dollar amount. However, I will say that the $1.6 trillion tax cut and tax rate flattening George W. Bush proposed at the beginning of his administration would have profited me somewhat more than it would most people. That should give you the ballpark range (it's also not an endorsement of that particular tax cut, incidentally).)

This document is going to be in Q & A format, with questions arranged in the order they come into my mind. Therefore there's a possibility this document will be somewhat disjointed and rambling. These are the risks you take. Buckle in.

1. I want to be a writer. What do I do?
DUH. You write, dummy.

2. No, no. I mean, I want to write professionally.
Oh, well, that's a totally different thing.

Let's be clear. Anyone who is even marginally literate can be a writer—all it takes is the desire to express yourself and the means to do it. One of the fairly neat things about the online medium, for example, is that it allows people to easily express themselves in writing to a bunch of other people, in the form of online journals and other such things. Even those folks who don't have such exhibitionist streaks can still sit down with a paper journal or even just a clean sheet of paper and write out their thoughts. There is no great science to being a writer; as I said earlier, you simply write. And hopefully you enjoy the process.

Writing professionally is something else again. The vast majority of the time, when you're writing professionally, you're not writing for yourself, you're writing for an audience—specifically (most of the time) an editor who is looking for writing of a certain nature or function, and in a more general sense, a larger readership that is looking for something specific: a technical document or a science fiction story or a poem or a recipe or some erotica or a movie review or an investigative report on tires or whatever.

You may from time to time hear the line from writing instructors that one should always write for one's self, but I think that's just a load of crap when it comes to writing for money. A lot of times when it comes to professional writing, you may be writing something you have absolutely no personal interest in whatsoever—you're writing what you're writing for someone else who has a specific need for the content you create. This is not to say you shouldn't have an interest in doing a good job or creating eminently readable content no matter what the context. It *does* mean that when you are writing professionally, you need to be aware of who your intended audience is and what they're looking for.

Or, to put it more succinctly: Writing professionally is a business. If you want to write professionally, you have to approach writing in a professional manner—which is to say, you have to approach it with the intent of actually making money doing it.

This means:

One: It takes work. Lots and lots and lots of work.

Two: Sometimes, work sucks.

Three: But you do it anyway because that's your job.

The previous three rules, incidentally, work for all writers, whether they write on staff or write freelance.

3. But I don't want to write stuff I don't want to write.

Then don't become a professional writer. Keep being a waiter or executive or student or bum or whatever you do now and work on the Great American Novel (or anything else it is you want to write) on the weekends. There's no reason you can't write and do something else that pays the bills at the same time (I'll be coming back to this concept more than once) and just write whatever you want.

That crack about writing the Great American Novel on the weekends isn't really a crack, either, since that's exactly how I wrote my first novel. Writing on the weekends actually can work. My point is, if you just wanna write what you just wanna write, don't make writing your profession—make it a side gig or an avocation or a hobby. Nothing wrong with that, honest.

If you want to make writing your profession, accept the fact that it's going to be easier to make a living as a writer if you're open to doing writing work that isn't romantic and appealing and exciting, but needs to be done anyway, and needs to be done to certain specifications that you may not have any personal interest in at all—i.e., accept that sometimes writing isn't this holy and uplifting thing we've all hoped it would be, but just a damned *job*. Accept it, deal with it, and do it—and do a good job.

Writers—professional writers, even—apparently have a hard time dealing with this. I'll let you in on a secret: One of the primary reasons I am as successful as I have been as a professional writer is I don't take my frustrations out on my clients and editors. My clients and editors tell me that one of the things they absolutely freakin' hate about writers is that they'll ask a writer to do something in a certain way, and the writer just won't listen. He or she will want to do it another way, and will then get all pissy and moody when they're told "no." Because they're *creative*, you see. They have this *vision*. And it should be *respected*.

No. No. *No.*

Not that I mind, of course. It just means more work for me, since I listen to my clients and I have no ego about the writing process—save doing the job that needs to be done, and doing it right and quickly. I let the client know that I have opinions, and I offer them if they're interested, but when they're not, I don't take it personally. It's a job. It needs to be done.

Look. This isn't to say that you can't get professional work only writing what you want, and that you can't ever get writing work without sacrificing this idea of writing as a sacred mission. People do it. But typically, these people also eat a lot of Top Ramen, especially when they're starting out. And Top Ramen sucks after the fifth or sixth day (trust me). Making a living writing will be a lot easier if you're ready to approach writing as a business rather than (or at least in tandem with) a life mission. Suffering for one's art is all very romantic, except when it's actually happening to you.

4. You're just trying to scare us all off of writing.
Yeah, *that's* it.

No, actually, it is—in the sense that I think those who want to be writers should have no illusions about the career track they want to engage in. People who aren't writers tend to think that those of us who are, are just farting around all day, then bang out some text in fifteen minutes and then go out for coffee. Maybe other writers do that, but I sure as hell don't (for one thing, I don't drink coffee). I *work*, damn it. I work hard, I work a lot, and I do a lot of writing that's not typically what you'd call "fun."

Yes, it's my personal choice to do it, one that's not going to be right for everyone. But the compensation, monetarily and in terms of personal lifestyle, is worth it. And it's been my experience that those writers who have an outlook similar to mine tend to do better (i.e., make more money) than those who don't. Take it or leave it.

**5. Okay, we got it—writing professionally
is endless pain and suffering.**

Well, no. Sorry to sound so strident. Writing profession-ally, even at its worst, still beats the hell out of lifting heavy objects off the back of a loading dock for $10 an hour. Let's not kid ourselves, here: It's not a hard life, relative to what other people have to do. This is no doubt part of the reason so many people want to be professional writers.

And I don't want to give the impression that I don't enjoy myself writing professionally. I like most all the writing I get paid to do. Some of it is more creative than other parts of it, but most of it is interesting, and that which is not isn't unbearable—indeed I find it relaxing and enjoyable because the process of writing it is interesting in itself. I like most of my clients and editors, too. The vast majority of them are normal, reasonable people who are just trying to do their own jobs as best they can. Work doesn't have to automatically mean "drudgery" and a Dilbert-like corporate Hell mentality. It really is a matter of how you approach it.

To sum up this rather long-winded portion: Writing professionally is actual work, for better and worse. If you can accept this fact, you'll be better off mentally to do well as a professional writer.

**6. Fine. I'm mentally prepared for being
a professional writer. Now how do I do it?**

Well, okay. Let me make the following assumption here: That, in fact, you can write your way out of a paper bag. If you're not sure you can actually, you know, *write*, you have no business trying to be a professional writer—go practice or take a class or do whatever that you need to do so you feel comfortable actually putting your work out there for other people to see. This is not the document in which I bolster your fragile ego and affirm your status as a real live writer. Go deal with that yourself. Somewhere else. Preferably away from me.

I'm also making the following assumption: You're just starting out. Because, really, if you're already a professional writer, you know all this stuff by now. Right? *Right?*

Okay. Let's start with beginning writer strategy number one, which works well for everyone, but especially those who want to be freelance writers:

a) First, buy a *Writer's Market*. This is your Bible, Koran and Torah from now on. This book features just about every single market for writing that exists.

b) Write an article on whatever you want to write about.

c) Open up your *Writer's Market,* find a magazine or other market that buys articles on the subject you've written on, format your article to that market's specifications, and send it off with a cover letter and an SASE (the *Writer's Market* will tell you how to do all this).

d) Forget about the article until it is either accepted or rejected.

e) Repeat steps a) - d) *ad infinitum.*

Alternately, you can switch steps c) and b) by finding markets that publish the sorts of articles you may be interested in writing, and then writing those articles according to their specifications. It's really up to you. The point is—start writing, start sending out articles, and keep at it.

(You can give your material a slightly better chance of being accepted if you at least initially write articles on a subject you know something about; for example, if you're a veterinarian, write articles about pets. If you love to knit, write articles about knitting. If you're an accountant, write about changes in the tax laws. And so on.)

(Bear in mind that some magazines and sites prefer to be queried first—that is, they want a proposal for an article rather than an article itself. This is not difficult to do, and again, your *Writer's Market* can show you how to do this. If a market wants a query, give them a query—don't annoy them by not paying attention to their requirements.)

Here's why this approach is useful: First, it gets you used to writing on a regular basis. Second, it gets you used to sending out material and continuing to send it out (and sending it out according to specifications—don't ignore this since editors throw out anything that's not to format specifications. No joke. You may think it doesn't matter, or that you're a special case, but you know what? You're *wrong*). Third, once you've started sending out work, assuming you're not an entirely incompetent writer, sooner or later someone is likely to accept something, and you can use that writing clip to help you get more work.

(What's beginning writer strategy number two? Show up at a local newspaper (that would be a dinky little paper, not like the *Los Angeles Times* if you live in LA) and offer your services as a writer and reporter, cheap. They may throw you some demeaning crap no one else wants to touch and gradually move you up from there. This technique is useful if you want to work as a journalist, as it will get you used to how a newsroom works, what deadlines are all about, and what sort of crap journalists have to put up with day in and day out—which includes but is not limited to bad pay, a shrinking market and the ever-present specter of being bought-out, replaced, or shut down. It's actually a lot of fun once you get used to it.)

Now, let's answer some questions here.

7. What if I send something out and it gets rejected?

What do you mean *"if"*?

Take this now and engrave this in your brain: **EVERY WRITER GETS REJECTED. You will be no different.** The rejection is not personal. Unless he or she mentions something specifically about it, the editor is not rejecting you as a human being or your right to exist on this planet. He or she is merely rejecting an article you've submitted. That's all. That's it.

If you can't handle the idea of rejection, you're really in the wrong line of work. It's just part of the business.

Articles get rejected for the following reasons:

a) They're not suitable for the magazine or site, i.e., you didn't do your homework and submitted something off topic for the magazine. This is a rookie error and why you should buy and actually read your *Writer's Market*, you dumbass.

b) They're on topic, but not of sufficient quality.

c) They're on topic, and of sufficient quality, but the magazine already recently ran something like it or has another article like it in the pipeline. This happens not infrequently.

d) It's on topic, of sufficient quality, and the magazine hasn't run something like it before, but the editor is simply a butthead and doesn't want to buy it. This also happens not infrequently.

e) Everything is perfect and the editor loves it, he or she just has no place for it right now.

When an article is rejected by an editor, don't assume it's crap. Just find another market that accepts articles along its line, and send it out again. And when it gets rejected again, send it out again. And so on and so on until either someone buys it or you run out of places to send it to. Only then do you toss it out or put it aside to try again at some other time.

8. Should I send material out to the big, big markets, even if I'm just getting started?

I don't see why not. The worst they can do is say no, and if they don't say no, you've made a sale to a big market—something you can use as ammo when selling articles to other places. And the big markets typically pay better, too, so that's always a benefit.

However, be aware that the bigger and better paying sites get correspondingly larger piles of submissions, so it's automatically a lot tougher to place material. Theoretically many of these markets are open to beginning writers, but there's a big difference between theory and practice. Sending an article to big markets may do nothing more than keep you from sending the article some place you might actually have a chance of being accepted. You need to decide whether it's worth the time.

9. Hey, an editor tells me that he'll accept my article if I make a couple of changes. What should I do?

DUH. Make the changes. An editor knows his magazine or site, and unless it drastically changes the thrust of the story (i.e., turns it from a positive to a negative review, for example, or turns you from a conservative to a flaming liberal), there's very little point in being difficult.

This last piece of advice is a lot more difficult to take if it's a creative or fiction piece, but suck it up and deal with it. Remember: When you're writing professionally, you're writing for an editor somewhere along the line. Editors exist (so far as you know) to ask for random and inexplicable changes to your work, and in return, they give you money. That's the drill.

10. I've sold an article! I've sold two!
Should I quit my day job?
Hell, no. Don't be an ass.

People who want to be writers look on their current jobs like they're chaining them down. If only they could break free of these jobs! Then they could write all the time! And be free! Oh joy!

Crap on a stick. Fact: Most people couldn't write all the time, even if they were free to do so. Even full-time writers (i.e., reporters and such) aren't writing every single moment of the work day; they're doing other stuff, including (yes) avoiding writing—because once writing is actual work, one desires to run away from it from time to time. I sure as hell don't write all the time, and this is my day job.

Another fact: Most writing pays for crap (more on this soon). Quitting your day job to write full time, especially if you're writing freelance, means you take a HUGE salary drop, no matter how little you're making now. And if you're just starting off, it's hard to make sales—so you'll be doubly screwed.

My suggestion: If you're starting off as a freelance writer, do it in your spare time—after work and on weekends. Don't ditch your day job to become a writer; let your day job support you as you work on perfecting your craft. It's a risk-free way of building that writing career (also, if the writing career doesn't pan out, you don't have to come crawling back at reduced pay and status). Most beginning freelancers don't have enough work to keep them busy anyway—they just spend most of their time worrying about how the hell they're going to pay their bills.

But, I hear you say, that's extra time I'm working! Yeah? So? If you weren't working on writing in the evenings what would you be doing? Watching *Friends*, or *Survivor* or playing video games or some crap like that. Yeah, you've *got* the time, pal. You just have to decide you want to do it.

So, when should you quit your day job? This is easy: You should quit your day job no earlier than when the amount of money you regularly and consistently make from writing exceeds your current day job income by 30%. That's right, you ought to be making *more* as a writer than you do from your day job in order to quit.

Why? Because the minute you quit your day job, you lose your employee benefits, your 401(k), and your employer contribution to your social security taxes. You have to pay for all of that yourself now. The minute you become self-employed as a freelancer, your tax burden jumps at least 15% (self-employment tax, don't you know), and you have to file quarterly.

You have to earn at least 30% more than what you make from your day job in order to live like you do off your day job income. This can be ameliorated somewhat if you have a spouse or significant other whose health insurance or benefits you can latch onto, but no matter what, you're still taking a big hit.

Here's the deal: Unless you're working at Burger King getting people their fries, you probably won't make as much writing as you do at your day job. So unless the thought of continuing work at your day job fills you with such a suicidal horror that you want to slit your wrists the moment you slip into your cubicle, don't quit. And if you do quit your day job, think about getting a *different* day job that has all those cushy benefits and 401(k)s, one that *doesn't* make you want to perforate your skull with a power nailgun.

Don't ever quit your day job unless not quitting your day job starts cutting into your total income potential. Really, that's what you should consider.

Remember also that many famous writers wrote books and columns and whatnot while holding down day jobs. Grisham and King had day jobs (lawyer and teacher, respectively). Scott Adams kept his cubicle job until he was a millionaire. Wallace Stevens, a Pulitzer Prize-winning poet and my personal favorite example of day-job-ness, was an insurance executive until the day he died. And so on. Day jobs don't keep you from writing. In fact, in a lot of cases, a day job can keep you writing, building your craft and your clip file while keeping you and your family fed.

Give it serious thought before you let your day job go.

11. What's this about writers being paid for crap?

It's the sad truth. Typically writers get paid crap for their contributions to magazines and web sites. This is especially true for freelancers (actually, salaried writers, on a per word basis, also don't get paid so hot. But they get dental and stuff, so that makes up for it). Crack open your *Writer's Market* and you'll notice that most magazines pay 20 cents a word or less for articles, and often much less—and if you're writing fiction, this pay scale drops dramatically.

Online sites are even more stingy; even top online sites like *Salon* pay only as well as mid-range print magazines or newspapers (don't even *think* of selling fiction online for actual money). If you're writing poetry, you can pretty much forget ever getting paid more than beer money, online or off.

Yes, there are a number of magazines that pay $1/word or more, but (no offense) your chances of getting into one of them as a new writer are pretty damn slim.

Okay, but what if you get a job as a real-life reporter or journalist? Heh. Starting journalist pay is in the low 20s, and that includes for grads of Northwestern and other prestigious journalism schools. That's as of 1999, and trust me, that number hasn't moved much for years. I know this because my first full-time job at the *Fresno Bee* paid me $24,000 in 1991—and that was so far down the pay scale that on a week-by-week basis, they had summer interns getting paid more than me the first year I was there. Also bear in mind that most of the "best" starting salaries for journalists come at the larger papers—if you're at a small local daily, you can expect rather substantially less.

From low beginnings, journalism salaries reach—well, not exactly great heights. If you work in a large city and you have several years of experience under your belt, you can reach somewhere in the $50k to $80k range, but again, most journalists aren't working in big city newsrooms; their salaries are somewhat smaller: in the 30s and 40s for long-time writers. Again, this ain't bad, especially when you factor in benefits, but relative to other professionals, like lawyers and doctors and MBAs, this is manifestly lower.

Now, there was a brief shining moment when online sites pushed journalist salaries into the $80k and $90k range, and even starting writers were making $50k. But then investors starting asking when these sites were going to start making money, and when it became clear they weren't, all those nice journalists with their nice sky-high salaries suddenly found themselves laid off. You won't see those levels again anytime soon.

Here's a spot of good news: Once you've done your time and developed a reputation as a really good writer, you can see your income go up—way up. Really. But it does take time, you really do have to do the work, and you really do have be good. You also have to work like a dog. However, until such time as that happens, you'll need to resign yourself to lousy pay no matter how you slice it.

(Bear in mind that none of this applies if you write for the *Harvard Lampoon*. In that case, you start making $360,000 a year as a writer on some sitcom as soon as you graduate. That Ivy League education is paying off!)

(Hey, yeah, I hear you say, what about screenwriters and TV writers? They get paid a lot! Well, yes, some of them do—most of them, however, *don't*. At all. And unless you're already in Hollywood, sliding your script to a producer under a bathroom stall with a vial of coke as a bribe, you're probably already too late. Sorry.)

Why is writer pay so low? Supply and demand. There are more people who are writers, and who want to be writers, than there are writing slots to be filled, either in terms of articles or in terms of staff positions. This is of course especially true at the bottom, where as a starting writer you will be. Near the top, as previously mentioned, things clear out a bit. But it's a long way from bottom to top. In this regard, it should be noted, writing is no different than any other desirable business field, although the entry-level pay sucks more than most. Only actors and musicians get paid less and exploited more.

There's also the matter of the writer "mystique" which works to the detriment of writer's pay—simply put, so many people are so desperate to be able to call themselves "writers" that they're willing to put up with low pay or even no pay in order to have that coveted title. This is again due to the idea that being a writer means you're part of something greater than yourself, that it's a calling, that your voice is being heard by the masses, blah blah blah, crap crap crap. Since you've got a lot of people who are writing-proficient willing to put up with lousy awful terrible pay, writing pay remains terrible.

Bear in mind that it's not only con artists who follow this theory: The *New York Times* famously pays a pittance to contributors to its op-ed pages, on the theory, presumably, that they should be honored to appear in the pages and spread their message to the World's Most Literate Audience. Yeah, whatever.

Again, this is a compelling reason not to quit your day job, since whatever day job it is almost certainly pays more than you'll be able to make from writing for the first few years—even if writing was the only thing you did.

12. Well, if writers get paid crap, how come you apparently make so damn much? You're not, like, *famous* or anything.

Excellent question.

Reason Number One: I've been writing professionally since 1990. Years of writing does count for something. Also bear in mind that for the first six years of writing professionally, I wasn't making that much at all—a newspaperman's salary during a recession (it wasn't bad, just not a lot). After that, I benefited to some extent from the wage inflation within the dotcom industry, and currently I'm benefiting from a decade's worth of contacts within the industry and a solid track record of output all that time (i.e, I'm not generally known for being a flaky, temperamental sort, at least when it comes to work). So there you have it: Time and effort count.

Reason Number Two: As a writer, I'm very flexible: I have significant experience in a whole bunch of different writing areas. Writing isn't just "writing," after all—just as doctors or lawyers specialize, so do most writers. This is generally an excellent strategy, but it's also worth your while as a writer to expand your reach once you've developed a core competence. In my own case, I started off writing entertainment and humor, which lead to my position at AOL.

While there, I got experience writing on online issues and also business-oriented writing, both in terms of personal finance and in terms of marketing. Those sidelines have since become an important part of my writing repertoire, enough so that while I am still actively involved in writing entertainment, it's now more of a sideline to these other sorts of writing.

More importantly, I'm still adding to my repertoire—I wrote a book on astronomy, for example, which will add more opportunities to write in the area of popular science. This range is useful to have, because when one sort of writing slows down, there are still opportunities to find work in other areas. So as a writer, flexibility helps quite a bit.

Reason Number Three: I'm not a writing snob. I won't just write certain types of writing—I'm a slut, I'll write anything if you pay me. This is related to being flexible, quite obviously, and it's also rooted in my desire to try different things. For example, some of my most profitable writing gigs involve writing marketing materials. A fair number of writers get snippy about writing marketing stuff, but you know what? I actually think it's kind of *fun*. It's fun to try a new medium of writing, it's fun to set a goal and try to hit it, it's fun to learn how this stuff works. And of course, writing marketing material pays really well, so it's also fun to spend the money I make off it. Some writers may hold up their noses at my largely indiscriminate writing proclivities, but that's fine. More work for me, more money for my family.

So if you want to make what I make—do your time, learn to write a lot of different things, and don't turn down work just because it's not "cool." See how easy it can be?

(Ironically, even "famous" writers don't make tons of cash. Sure, you've got King and Grisham and Rice and so on, and there's a nice patrician class of opinion columnists and what have you who are socking the bucks away. But that's the top 1%. Below that the upper ranks are comfy but not cushy. Even lower-rung best-selling authors aren't notably rich—when your royalty rate is 10% or less, you have to sell a lot of books to see any real money at all (trust me on this). Well-known national columnists, while making more than the average Joe writer, don't get paid excessively either: high five figures or very low six figures. You can have a nice income if you're a writer (eventually), but if you want to be really super duper *ultra* rich, you might want to try being famous in some other line of work.)

13. Don't you worry you'll spend so much time writing for others that you'll never write the stuff you want to write for yourself?

Every now and then, sure. And to be very clear, I do think it's *extremely* important for writers to make sure they do some writing that's actually important to them. Because if all you do is write for other people, you'll probably become crabbed and irritable and no damned fun to be around. Writing what one enjoys keeps one mentally fresh—and it's fun besides.

The important thing is to find the balance of writing for work and writing for one's own personal enjoyment, and it's something that can take some time to figure out. Certainly I'm guilty from time to time of piling so much work on my plate that I don't have time for fun writing, and when that happens I end up feeling moderately miserable until I'm in a place where I've got all that work cleared out (on the other hand, if I didn't have paid writing work to do, you can bet I'd be pretty damned miserable then, too).

In my own personal experience, I've found that I'm happiest when I have a healthy amount of paid work and a couple hours a day to do personal writing. The reason for this is I tend to be "creative" a couple of hours a day, after which point my brain needs some time to rest, recharge and think about whatever it is I'm writing creatively. So for the rest of the day, I do my paid work. The two don't interfere with each other, and indeed can complement each other, with what I'm doing creatively causing me to approach my paid work from a slightly different perspective and vice-versa. And of course, much of your "personal" writing can also have professional goals—if you're writing a novel, for example, you'll probably want to try to sell it after you're done.

Your ratio of professional to personal work and the set up of how you write both will be different then mine, obviously. You'll figure it out eventually. In the meantime, I wouldn't advise obsessing about whether you're losing your soul by writing too much stuff for other people and not enough for yourself. When it comes right down to it, if you really want to make the time for personal writing, you'll do it.

14. Is there anything you wouldn't write for money?

You bet. I wouldn't ever write marketing material for a product I found morally questionable, so, for example, no sweet rich cigarette money for me. I wouldn't write anything counter to my own political or personal ethics, so this means you won't see me writing direct mail for conservative politicians, warning their constituents about the evils of, say, gay marriage or pro-choicers. I won't write in a medium that I find personally offensive, which means you are unlikely to find me writing unsolicited e-mail marketing pieces. I'm unlikely to write porn, because I couldn't write it without busting up. I wouldn't write anything that I felt I clearly lacked the knowledge base for or, alternately, felt I wouldn't be able to pick up quickly enough to turn out a reasonable product. So there goes my career writing about cricket.

Bear in mind that I say this feeling relatively comfortable that saying "no" to any of these sorts of writing would not impact my overall ability to make a living and pay my bills. If I were a beginning writer and writing an unsolicited e-mail marketing piece meant the difference between eating Top Ramen or eating real food for a change, I might cave. But in a general sense, life's too short to do things that make you feel dirty or vaguely ashamed of yourself. There are other ways to make money.

15. Hey, you mentioned earlier that you had contacts in the industry. How did you get them? And more to the point, how can *I* get them?

"Contacts" is a term which calls into mind shadowy types that have mystical powers to get you writing gigs and hot dates with supermodels. It's not like that all, especially the part about the hot dates. My contacts are just all the people I've met along the way. Most of these people I met when both they and I were younger and in positions far less advantageous than the ones we're both in now. Over time, people move up, and they remember people they've worked with before. That's pretty much how it works.

If you're interested in cultivating contacts of your own for fun and profit, here's what you do: **Be nice to everyone.** Really, that's the best way to do it. When you work with someone, help them do their job (usually this is accomplished simply by doing your own job in a competent manner). Don't adopt a superior attitude to anyone—you'll be surprised how quickly today's peon becomes tomorrow's boss (and how long their memories are). Thank people when they're helpful. Be useful. Don't talk about them behind their backs. Don't stab them in the back. If you think someone is good at his or her job and you're in a position to help them advance, do it. People do remember those who have done well by them, both professionally and personally. Being a decent human being pays off.

Being nice, incidentally, is not the same as being an ass-kissing yes-man. Insincerity has a pungent stench that will hang about you all your career, so be careful about using it. One can be generally nice and still not roll over and take it up the wazoo from some crap-flinging monkey of a co-worker or editor. Related to this, you should have a certain line beyond which you will take no more crap from anyone, nor let anyone take additional advantage of you. This line is useful for one's self-respect and one's ability to do work. No job in the world is worth taking more than one's fair share of crap. However, my experience has been that most people are in fact normal folks just trying to do their job. If you help them do it, and do so in a pleasant, professional and engaging way, it'll pay dividends.

(Also remember that being the nicest person in the world won't mean a thing if you can't, you know, actually *do* the job. So work on your professional chops first, and on being nice second.)

16. I have no contacts! I know no one! What should I do?

Please refer to beginning writer strategy number one back at question number six. Look, people, *not* having contacts doesn't mean you'll never get work. I didn't know anyone at the first four major writing gigs I had; the only thing I had going for me was the work I was able to show them. *Work counts.* It counts at least as much as contacts, especially at the beginning.

17. What do you think about writer's unions, associations and conventions?

I'm officially neutral on them. I think they can be very useful for new writers in learning many of the ground rules of writing as a career, and can be especially helpful when legal or contractual matters crop up. Local writer associations are useful as social and professional entities as well. Additionally, many national and local writers unions and associations offer useful benefits to members, such as health insurance. This alone can make joining a very good thing for freelance writers.

However, personally speaking, I've found very little use for them. For whatever reason, I've had very few problems negotiating contracts on my own or finding suitable work, both as a full-time salaried worker and a full-time freelancer, and I've not had problems meeting and cultivating contacts. Writing conventions and seminars haven't been very useful to me; typically I find a much more useful experience is simply to go out and get the actual professional experience in whatever field I'm curious about. And also, I'm cheap and I refuse to spend money for dues unless I feel I'm personally going to receive a direct net benefit. While I'm politically pro-union in a general sense, on a personal level I'm apparently not at *all*.

The above should be read with the understanding that I am exceptionally egotistical and confident in my abilities to the point of being irritating to other writers, and also that I tend not to be a "joiner" of organized groups. The only writing organization I had any ambition to join is the Science Fiction and Fantasy Writers of America, of which I am now a member. I didn't actually expect it to do anything for me when I joined, and to that extent I have been not at all disappointed with its performance. I get to vote on the Nebula awards, though, and that's nice.

So: If you think it's going to be useful to you, join a writer's union. I personally have not found them useful, but that's not the same thing as saying you won't find them so.

18. You write online and offline.
What are the differences between them?
There are none.

I'm serious. A lot of people talk about how different the two mediums are, but it's mostly wishful thinking. Online writing tends to be shorter, and it has the ability to take advantage of hyperlinking, which print cannot. But that's it, and, in both of these cases, it's not a hard and fast rule, since I've read lots of Web writing which is not notably short, and a lot of articles that did not include hyperlinks. Lots of writers who work online also learn HTML or other web-based presentation systems, but that's not directly related to writing *per se*. One can get along perfectly well without learning it, especially these days, when word processing programs can format your text as a Web page for you.

In both the online and offline mediums, you ultimately have to do the same things—you have to write coherently and intelligently, and you have to make your editor happy. If you can write in one medium, you know 95% percent of what you need to know to work in the other, and what little there is that is different is not difficult to learn.

A number of writers I know seem to prefer to work in only one medium and not the other. I think that's kind of dumb. Inasmuch as there's no real skill set difference between two, why not write in both? Woody Allen once joked that the great thing about being bisexual is that it doubled your chances of a date on Saturday night; the same thinking applies to offline and online writing. Currently (2001), my income is derived 75% from online work, 25% from offline. I'm not willing to chop off a quarter of my income (or three quarters, if I go the other way) in some misguided belief that one needs to concentrate on one medium rather than the other.

(Why is my income majority online, you ask? It's simple—I'm lazy, and online work is easier for me to find, thanks to contacts and online job banks. However, were the online world to vaporize tomorrow, I don't have any doubt I could begin building up my income writing offline, using writing skills and experiences I cultivated in my online writing.)

19. Do I have to go to New York or some other large city to write? That's where most of the writing opportunities seem to be located.

Oh, I don't know about that. Certainly the highest-profile magazines and writing outlets are in New York and other large cities. But magazines are located all over the map. And unless you're submitting to a region-oriented magazine or want to work for a local newspaper, you typically don't have to live where the writing market is located. Yes, there's something to be said about being able to have face time with editors and magazine and newspaper staffs, but it's not absolutely essential.

I think you should move to a large city to write if you actually want to move to a large city, period. If not, don't. Living in one particular place to write is becoming less necessary, especially now that the online world means people are just an e-mail or instant message away from each other. I speak about this with some experience; I currently live in a dinky little town on the far western edge of Ohio called Bradford—population just under 2,000. When I moved here I was worried that living here would have some impact on my ability to get work, but it really hasn't at all. I may be lucky in this regard, but I think anyone who is committed to finding writing work these days can find it no matter where they live.

Now, if I were 21 and just starting out, I'd much rather live in New York than Bradford, Ohio. Oh. MY. *God*. There's no debate on this. But now I'm in my thirties and I have a family, I'd rather live here. I have a brand-new 4-bedroom house on five acres of land, and what I pay monthly on the mortgage wouldn't even get me a crappy one-bedroom in Manhattan. My kid gets to play in a yard the size of a New York city block, which (for me, at least) seems like a better idea than her actually playing on a New York city block. No offense to New Yorkers.

Point here: You can write from anywhere, especially these days. So live where you want.

20. I'm a college student who wants to grow up to be a writer. What classes should I take?

Take whatever you want. If you know you want to be a writer, then you'll probably write at every opportunity anyway; taking classes on how to write is of secondary utility to actually writing. Given the choice between a class on writing and, say writing for the college newspaper, I'd suggest writing for the college newspaper and freeing up that class time for something else. Professors and other writing teachers may disagree, but you know what? I make more than almost *all* of them. Who are you going to believe. Now, if you have no clue how to put a sentence together, best hie yourself to a writing class, and that damned quick. But most people who really want to write tend to have that bit down.

Far more important than sitting around discussing your writing quirks with other students is actually learning as much as you can about as many things as you can. Why?

Because having a wide range of knowledge makes you a better writer—it makes you more able to write about a number of topics, and it allows you to make connections between disparate fields of knowledge and thus uncover new ideas (which you can then write about). It also makes you look more intelligent to the men/women you want to impress. But most of all, learning about a bunch of different things teaches you how to learn—an utterly invaluable skill when it comes to writing, which often requires a lot of research and/or the ability to quickly learn stuff about a subject as you go along.

One of the things that they never tell you in high school is that your undergraduate college degree doesn't count for a whole hell of a lot—if you're going to be a professional worker of any sort, you typically do more work on the subject in graduate school, and these grad schools like to have a nice range of students. This is why you'll often see English under-grads in MBA programs and biology majors in law school. If you want to pursue writing on an academic level—which really is optional for a professional writing career and not at all necessary if you actually go and do real writing for real magazines and newspapers and such like (ahem) I did—there are several very good graduate writing programs, and of course tons of journalism schools. All of these take students who have all sorts of undergrad majors. Worry about it then—and in the meantime use your undergraduate years to learn a lot about a lot. It'll pay off in the long run.

(My major? Philosophy. Have I ever used it profes-sionally? Yeah, right.)

Okay, I'm done talking now.

EVEN MORE LONG-WINDED (BUT PRACTICAL) WRITING ADVICE

(March 19, 2004)

For various reasons which I will not go into at the moment because I don't feel like it, I have the urge to provide wholly unsolicited but practical advice to writers. So here it is. Why should you as a writer listen to my advice? No reason except that I published two books last year, will publish two books this year and am likely to publish another couple of books next year, and aside from that I make a whole lot of money doing what I do. On the other hand, I am also famously a cranky blowhard who readily admits to having his head up his ass a lot of the time. So take it or leave it.

1. Yes, you're a great writer. So what.

Let's be clear on this, so there's no confusion on that matter: no one cares that you're totally the best writer ever. They just don't. Because while people want their writers to be many things, "the best" isn't usually one of those things. Readers want you to be entertaining. Editors want you to have commercial appeal and not be a pain in the ass to line edit. Publishers want you to fill a hole in their production schedule. Book stores want you to stimulate foot traffic in their store. None of that inherently has anything to do with being a great writer. If you can do one or more of these things and be a great writer, nifty. If being a great writer keeps you from doing these things, well, pal, expect to be deeply underappreciated in your time. Somewhat related to this:

2. I don't care if you're a better writer than *me*.

Because why should I? Yes, words drip from your pen like liquid gold skittering across the finest vellum ever pounded out of a lamb. Trees weep with gratitude that their deaths afford you the paper upon which you will cast your thoughts. That's *very* nice for you. Meanwhile, I've got my own books to write, projects to develop and clients to make happy. Your preternatural ability to weave filigreed musings into deathless prose impacts my life not at all.

I of course accept your superiority to me in the great hierarchy of writers—clearly, confronted with your brilliance, how could I not? I just don't *care*. Unless you intend to spend all your time trying to thwart my career because you can't bear to contemplate my muddy work sullying the field of endeavor over which you float, carried by the angels, simply as a *practical* matter what you do and what I do will have very little to do with each other.

I suspect my feeling here will be echoed by other writers. Be as brilliant as you want to be, friend. Just don't expect the rest of us to look up from our toil to stare agape as you waft by. And somewhat related to *this*:

3. There is always someone less talented than you making more money as a writer.

Why? Because life (and publishing) is capricious and cruel, that's why. Some fat bastard has been rewriting the same book for the last 25 years, and each "new" book is even more of a pointlessly smudged photocopy of his last book than the one before it, which in turn was a smudged photocopy of the book before *that*. And after his thick, retarded lummox of a book is planted in its own stand-up display smack in the middle of the store's primary traffic pattern, the author is going to take that money, buy a gorgeous house on Lake Tahoe with it and use the excess cash to charm smart, pretty, ambitious girls and boys to have rampaging sex with his flabby, liver-spotted body while he watches Nick Jr. on his 83-inch high-definition plasma television. Because he *can*. Meanwhile, you're lucky if a single copy of your achingly beautifully-written paperback, for which you were paid barely enough to cover three month's rent on a bug-infested Alphabet City 5th-floor walkup, is shelved spine inward in a forgotten limb of the bookstore for a month before its cover is amputated and sent back to the publisher as a mark of abject failure. Welcome to the literary world!

Just remember when that happens that someone else's retina-blindingly gorgeous manuscript—which is so much better than the tripe *you* write that you hardly deserve to know of its existence—lies neglected in a slush pile at a publisher, to be pawed over by a summer intern with as much taste in books as a heat-addled aardvark, before being returned 15 to 22 months after it was submitted. Yes, that's right: You're one of the *lucky* ones.

4. Your opinion about other writers (and their writing) means nothing.

In one of the comment threads on my Web site, a correspondent mentioned that another writer was telling her that no editor would ever buy my novels—and later that *very same day* I announced that I'd been signed to a two-novel deal, and that the books would be coming out in hardback. Why on this subject was this other writer so clearly and obviously wrong, *wrong*, **wrong?** Well, simple: Because he knows *nothing*—or at the very least, he knew nothing useful about the market in which these books would be in play. His *opinion* was that I was a bad writer and my books stank, but the reality was someone in a position to *buy* my work thought I was competent enough and the book good enough to purchase (and to justify another book purchase from me, sight unseen).

This is not to pound on this particular writer for knowing absolutely nothing about the market he was presuming to comment upon. Well, actually that's a lie: it *is*. But allow me to be the first to note that there are a lot of books out there—really successful books—that I wouldn't have given a snowball's chance in Hell of ever being published. And yet, there they are, selling millions. Why? Because *I* know nothing, too. As writers, our jobs are *not* to know anything about other writers and their work; our jobs are to work on our own writing.

This is not to say one can't have opinions about other writers and their work; we can. We all do. But we shouldn't bother pretending that our opinions have any relation to how that writer and his or her work will fare in the world. Speaking as a writer, and someone with an opinion, I don't need to validate my opinion by assuming it has a greater significance than being my own opinion. I have enough of an ego to feel that it merely being my opinion is good enough.

5. You're not fooling anyone when you take your laptop to a coffee shop, you know.

I mean, *Christ*, people. All that tapping and leaning back thoughtfully in your chair with a mug of whatever while you pretend to edit your latest masterpiece. You couldn't be more obvious if you had a garish, flashing neon sign over your head that said "Looking For Sex." Go *home*, why don't you. Just *go*.

Admittedly if everyone followed my advice the entire economy of Park Slope would implode. But look, do you want to write, or do you want to get laid? No, *don't* answer that. Anyway, if you *really* want to impress the hot whomevers, you'll bring your bound galleys to the coffeeshop to edit. That'll make the laptop tappers look like pathetic chumps. We're talking hot libidinous mammal sex for *days*.

6. Until you're published,
you're just in the peanut gallery.

This is regarding your thoughts on the publishing industry, mind you (you're still perfectly entitled to your opinions about what you like and don't like. I know, it's nice of me to let you have that, right?). And no, CafePress and the various Publish-on-Demand iterations don't count. There's nothing wrong with those, in my opinion, and of course I "published" my first novel on my own Web site, and I think that novel is perfectly good.

But it's not the same, because (among other things) if it *were* the same then people who get published that way wouldn't have to spend so much of their time defensively suggesting that it *is*. You have to be really published by someone who is going to pay you money up front, and then get walked through the secret handshake and all the mysterious Gutenbergian rituals, and that thing with the hot type pressed searingly into your trembling but willing flesh, before anyone who is published gives a *crap* about what you think (and even then they don't think much of it— see previous points).

Yes, it's snobbery. So what? You make it sound like snobbery is a *bad* thing. Anyway, not being published yet doesn't mean you're a bad writer, it just means you're not published yet. But writers feel about people spouting off about writing like Marines feel about civilians spouting off about the Corps; unless you've done your time, you're just farting through your larynx. Get published and then come back and tell us what you think about things.

7. Did I mention life's not fair?

Well, it's not. Take me. I got my first book sale because my agent thought of me when a publisher was looking for a particular kind of book. No effort required. Sold my first novel off of my Web site. Not much effort required there, either. Sold my second novel off a one-sentence pitch; see above (the *writing* of that novel, however, required a *lot* of effort). And now I've got myself a nice little book franchise with the *Book of the Dumb* books.

Lucky? Well, *duh*. However, it's worth mentioning that around the same time I sold my novel for a modest little sum, some 19-year-old named Christopher Paolini had his self-published fantasy book called *Eragon* snapped up by Knopf for $500,000; now it's a best seller and they're going to make a big expensive movie of it. So *I'm* lucky, but our young friend Paolini hit the friggin' *jackpot*.

Is it *fair* I have a book career through little effort of my own (aside from the trivial but necessary step of writing the books), while others of equal or greater talent plug away for years with no success? Nope. Is it fair that Paolini is a best-selling, fairly rich author at 20 years old while I have to wait until I'm 35 to have *my* first novel in the stores—and others have to wait even longer (if they ever get published at all)? A big fat "nope" to that one, too. Life isn't fair. It really never has been and it seems awfully naive to expect it to become that way anytime soon.

I am happy to grant that some of the success I have had has been a matter of being in the right place at the right time, but I don't feel obliged to feel guilty about taking advantage of that fortuitous positioning, since the end result is a good life doing what I want. And if you're in a position to take advantage of similar luck, you shouldn't feel guilty about it either. Chalk it up to an advance on your karmic balance; try not to screw it up.

8. Don't be an ass.

Did you know that writers, editors and publishers will forget their own names and the names of their children, spouses and pets before they forget the tiniest of slights that you as a fellow writer might inflict upon them? It's true. Verily, they could be in the throes of an advanced, prion-twisting affliction that wipes their memories clean like a Magna-Doodle in an MRI, and yet if your name is but whispered from across the room, their eyes will blaze and they will exclaim "that bastard!" before lapsing back into the blank darkness. That being the case, why would you go out of your way to antagonize these people unless it is *absolutely* necessary—which it almost never, ever is?

In this life, and in this field, you're going to have enough problems as it is. Don't make any more enemies than you have to. Try to be nice. And if you can't be nice, then shut the hell up and go stand in the corner with your drink and leave all the rest of us alone. Yes, yes, you're right and everyone else is wrong. That—like your immense talent—is a given. But just because you're *right* doesn't mean you should be a dick about it.

9. You will look stupid if you're jealous.

Just as there will be writers with more success and less talent than you, some of your writer friends will do better than you, by whatever standard you decide "better" counts as. And you know what you should do? Be happy for them, you neurotic twit. Because it's more than likely that their success has almost nothing to do with you—which is to say that if they were less successful, *you* would probably still be no more or less successful than you are. Life is not a zero-sum game; the fortunes of others do not mean our own fortunes are diminished. I mean, for God's sake, there are 280 million people in the United States. Do you *really* think the success of *one* of them in your field of work negates *your* ability to be successful? Jesus. A little self-centered, aren't we.

So, suck it up. Be happy for your friend. Not only is it what you're *supposed* to do as a friend, and thus its own very good reason, but it's also the way to make your friend get the idea that now that he or she is successful, they're going to go out of their way to help you. So if you can't be happy for your friend for his or her own sake—optimal—do it for the career opportunity it affords you—less optimal but we can't all be cheerleaders, can we.

(And if turns out you *are* the most successful among your writer friends, well, you know. Be a pal.)

Being jealous of people you don't even know, incidentally, is so rock-dense stupid that I'm going to pay you the compliment of assuming that *you* wouldn't do something as pointless as that. You're welcome.

10. Life is long.

So long as you don't intentionally step out in front of a bus, chances are pretty good you'll make it to 70 or 80 or some bone-deteriorated age like that. That being the case, what are you worried about? Enjoy yourself. Enjoy the process of writing. Revel in the joy of creating whatever it is you're creating and *don't worry*. For some people writing success happens early, for others later, and for most somewhere in between. Did I think I'd be in my 30s before I sold my first novel? No, but there's lots of things about my life I *didn't* expect—and since I can't imagine why I would want my life to be any different than it is, I guess that this is a *good* thing.

Life is long. You can write all the way through it; this ain't gymnastics, after all. Live life, do your writing, and get used to the idea that things happen when they happen. There's no timetable. There's just life, and any part of it can be as good a time as any other to be the writer you want to be.

I'm done.

If you'll note the date this one was published, you'll see why this particular piece got lost in the shuffle. A couple of the points I made here I later replicated in other pieces, but I thought it'd be nice to let this piece see the light of day once more. Also, there are some points here I don't make elsewhere. So there you are. —JS

TEN THINGS I'VE LEARNED ABOUT WRITING IN TEN YEARS OF DOING IT

(September 10, 2001)

This last week marked my tenth anniversary as a working writer. I wrote before that point, of course, and I even got paid for it from time to time, but I time my professional life from the date I walked in the door of the *Fresno Bee* in September of 1991 and said "I start work today." They gave me a photo ID, a desk and a paycheck (the paycheck actually came two weeks later. But you know what I mean). Ta da, I was a real live working writer.

Ten years later, I still haven't done anything else to make money—including during the last three and a half years, in which I've been a freelance writer, a sure second job magnet if there ever was one. My career has been a nice combination of being lucky and being good, and while I prefer being the latter, I don't turn my nose up at the former, either. I'm not proud. I'll take luck when I can get it.

However I've managed it, ten years of writing—on staff and freelance, for print, magazines, online and in books, and on just about every topic possible—is enough time to note some general observations about the writing life. So here they are: Ten Things I've Learned About Writing From Ten Years of Doing It. These are in no particular order, incidentally.

1. If you're not confident, you're dead meat.

Beyond the fact that whiny writers suck, being confident is your road to cash. I charge a hefty amount per hour and per word for my services, and the reason I can get away with it is this: When clients call with a project or article that is a ridiculous amount of work in a ridiculously short frame and they ask me if I can do it, I tell them the only thing they want hear: "Sure. No problem." Clients pay me for my writing skills, but they pay me a *lot* because I give them the security that the work is going to get done, period. If you can project that sort of confidence in your work—in the quality and in the timeliness—to your clients, it goes a long way to keeping you in work.

2. Nothing lasts forever.

In my time I've had a number of sweet writing gigs: reviewing movies and CDs and video games, writing humor columns and so on. They all come and they all go, and it very often has little to do with me personally—there's a decision in the upper ranks to cut content, or change the job description, or move the publication in another direction or whatever (of course, sometimes it *is* about me. But never mind that now). These can happen to you, too—and sometimes, God forbid, you just get tired of doing one particular thing. Whatever the reason, budget change into your writing life. If you ever land that sweet, sweet writing gig, the one that has you thinking *this is too good to last*—you're probably right. Hope it does last. Prepare for it not to.

3. Writers spend too much time obsessing about the people who don't respect them.

Yes, yes, yes. *Everyone* wants to screw the writer (except for the hot, beautiful people *we* want to screw, who won't give us the time of day)—no one respects us, no one pays us what we're worth, no one values our contribution, blah blah blah blah *blah*. Perhaps it's because writers are intelligent introspective folk, or maybe it's because they have no spines, but whatever the reason, writers spend far more time complaining about how they're getting screwed than they spend getting themselves out of the position of being screwed. Now, as a writer, I've been screwed from time to time. But to my credit, I typically only get screwed *once*.

I don't spend too much time railing about the injustices carried out upon writers *en masse* by the uncaring world. It's not that I'm insensitive to the plight of my fellow writers—really, I hope you all show up that lousy world one day—but more to the point that my experience has been that there *are* people who value good work from good writers, and I endeavor to work for them. As a writer and a worker, when I find myself in a position where I feel I'm getting screwed, I tend to vote with my feet. The reason I do this goes back to point #1 up there: I'm reasonably confident I can find work. You should be, too (the secret is to find work *before* you leave).

**4. You're not a real writer
until you write a book.**

By which I mean, *non-writers* are fairly unimpressed with you unless you have a book (or a screenplay made into a widely-released movie, and no, straight-to-video doesn't count). I mention to people that I'm a writer, and they ask what I've written. And I go down the list, and they start nodding off until I say, "and I have a book in the stores." At which point you can see the following thought behind their eyes: *So! He's not actually a bum after all!* Real, honest-to-goodness writers who toil year after year in the dusty fields of journalism or public relations or whatever might find this annoying and irritating, but, hey, I'm not saying this is fair. I'm just saying it happens. People understand "book = writer."

"Book," by the way, meaning *printed* book—no offense to e-book writers (I happen to be one myself), but if it's not on paper, no one but you counts it as a real book. Oh, and related to this:

5. You really do need an agent.

You're more likely to be eaten by a bull shark off the Florida Panhandle than to sell a book these days without one of these guys. So get one. Get a good one. Trust me.

**6. The secret to making money:
give in to the Man.**

Don't be proud, buster. If your aim in writing is to actually make money from time to time, particularly as a freelance writer, suck it up and write some ad copy. Or a financial brochure. Or a technical document. Or whatever. No, it's not the Great American Novel, but you know what, there can be only one Great American Novel, and the chances of

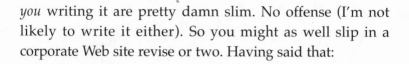

you writing it are pretty damn slim. No offense (I'm not likely to write it either). So you might as well slip in a corporate Web site revise or two. Having said that:

7. You damn well better make time for your "real" writing.

Making money hand over fist is all very nice, but, yes, it's true: You *do* need to budget time to write the sort of stuff that's important to you, or you *will* regret it—and then you'll probably make everyone you know regret it, too. And if there's one thing the world doesn't need, it's another depressed 55-year-old writer suddenly realizing that all he or she has to show for three decades of writing work is a stack of faxable press releases or archived city council articles. Yes, it's very sad you blew your wad on that alone. So if only as a preventative measure, to save those who love you from wanting to strangle your sorry ass, pencil in some time on the weekend for your novel.

8. Writing is romantic, but don't be romantic about writing.

Being able to say you're a writer is pretty cool, and gives you singles bar credibility that few other professions that hang out in singles bars can match. But aside from that perk, if you write for a living, and you're not thinking about writing as a business, you're pretty stupid. The three rules of writing:

1. It's Work.
2. It's Work.
3. Surprise! It's Work.

The hot young thangs you meet in a bar will think it's cool you're a writer, but they'll think it's even *more* cool if you can afford to take them on a date to a place where the food can't be "Super Sized."

9. Be fearless.

My writing career is based on a series of incidents where people have asked me if I could write on a particular subject, and I said, "Oh absolutely," and then I went off and learned about whatever the hell it was I was supposed to be writing on. This is not an exaggeration, by the way—my job at the *Fresno Bee* was as a movie critic, for which I had absolutely no experience and nothing to recommend me for the position except that I was good with them there words, and I was cheap (oh so *very* cheap. I was 22. What do you want).

I'm not dumb about this—I'm not going to be writing for a quantum physics journal, for example, since my math skills gave out some time around the quadratic equation—but at the same time, as a writer, I generally have no fear of things I don't know. I'm confident in my ability to learn (Thank you Webb and the University of Chicago), and I'm confident in my ability to communicate. Being fearless when it comes to writing has not just helped my career—fundamentally, it has *been* my career. Don't be afraid to jump into the deep end of the pool. Trust your writing chops, and trust yourself, and you'll be fine.

10. If you can live with your choices, you're a good writer.

From time to time I wonder if I've done the right thing with my writing career, which has been and continues to be a rather pixilated affair. But ultimately I'm pretty happy with where I am. I earn good money for my family. I write stuff that I enjoy, and I enjoy working with the people for whom I write. I have a good life that I live, for the most part, on my own terms. And while there's more that I want to do with my writing career, I can honestly say that I don't regret any of the choices I've made so far. As a writer, and as a working human being, that's what you hope for. If you can look at your own writing life and feel the same way, then whatever your choices so far, and whatever you want for yourself in the future, you're doing just fine in the here and now.

So there you have it, ten years of writing experience. Let's see what the next ten years has in store.

In early 2005 I was asked to guest-edit an issue of
Subterranean Magazine, *a science-fiction/fantasy maga-*
zine. After announcing my editorship, I posted this piece
to let people know how I was planning to handle the
inevitable spate of rejections that would ensue. It seems to
have worked—after the rejections were mailed out I got e-
mails thanking me for being so nice about it all. I try. In
any event, the piece described my own rejection policy, but
I think you'll find the advice about following directions
and how to deal with rejection applicable across a wide
range of submission events. I find it useful, in any event,
when I submit things. —JS

TEN THINGS
ABOUT
LITERARY REJECTION

(March 23, 2005)

Since I will be in the position of rejecting people's work later in the year, I wanted to post ten quick things about rejection that I think people should know, at least as it regards what I'll be doing.

1. If you haven't read book editor Teresa Nielsen Hayden's seminal "Slushkiller" entry about the editorial side of rejection, stop reading this and go read that instead. Right now (it's at **http://nielsenhayden.com/makinglight/archives/004641.html**). You will be enlightened, and if you're not, you probably shouldn't be writing. "Slushkiller" should be given to every single aspiring writer before he or she is allowed to submit a damn thing.

2. The magazine issue I'm editing will feature 12 to 30 articles totaling 60,000 words (more or less). I expect that I will receive *more* than 30 submissions and/or 60,000 words worth of material for my consideration. Therefore, I expect I will be rejecting a fair amount of material.

3. Writers who do not believe that submission guidelines should apply to them are going to be rather unpleasantly surprised when I disagree. I regard adherence to submission guidelines as an IQ test and assume those who cannot or will not follow them are no more likely to be able to write a good story than a fish can play a tuba. This may be unfair to the writer (and the fish), but not following my submission guidelines is unfair to *me* (and to other writers who *do* follow submission guidelines). So that makes us even in the unfairness department. This will weed out a surprising number of submissions. Try not to be one of them.

4. I read each story until it no longer works for me. If that happens before the end of the story, I'm going to reject the piece. I don't usually know from piece to piece what's going to work for me. Like pornography or a good melon, I know entertaining work when I see it. But I guarantee you if *you* think there's a point at which your story lags, *I* will, too. *Don't give me the opportunity to decide your piece doesn't work.* If the story works all the way through that doesn't mean it's accepted, but it does mean it'll make it into the pool of stories I'd *like* to buy.

5. I will almost certainly *not* be able to buy every single story I'd like to buy. I have finite space and I also have to consider balance for the magazine—I can't have three stories with the same plot device, even if all three pieces are heartbreakingly good. Therefore, some of the stories I will reject it will *kill* me to reject—but I'll have to reject them anyway, and hope that they find another home where they will be loved.

6. *You will not know why I rejected your work.* I intend to send out form rejections that will politely but briefly note that I will not be able to use the submission. I do not plan to explain the rejection. I recognize that people want to know why their work is rejected, but as a practical matter it would be difficult to individualize each rejection. If you'd like to assume that I loved the piece but was simply unable to put it in the magazine, that's groovy by me, since in several cases that will be the truth.

7. *I am rejecting the piece, not you.* As noted above, rejection happens for many reasons, and much good work that deserves publication is rejected for reasons that have little or nothing to do with the writing. The rejection of your submission is not a referendum on you as a human being, or even on you as a writer. It is simply acknowledging that for whatever reason, *this* piece does not suit *my* needs *at this time*. If you take rejection personally as a writer, you will go mad, because every writer gets rejected. A *lot*.

8. If it helps you to think that the reason I rejected your work is because I'm a fookin' idjit, I accept and celebrate that decision. Still, try to treat me kindly the next time we see each other.

9. If you were my best friend and you submitted a story I couldn't use, I would reject it. If you were my mother and you submitted a story I couldn't use, I would reject it. If you were Jesus at the right hand of God and you submitted a story I couldn't use, I would reject it. If you were my mortal, hated enemy who submitted a story that knocked me on my ass and fit perfectly with what I was trying to do, I would buy that story in a heartbeat. And then I'd hope you get hit by a bus. Point: The readers of the magazine couldn't possibly care what my relationship is to the writers. They just want a good read. My job is to make that happen.

10. Whether I reject your story or accept it, I will treat it as I would have my own work treated by another editor. I will assume that every story will work for me until I am persuaded otherwise. I will recognize that the work you've sent represents your best efforts. And I will remember that you honor me when you send in your work for my consideration. Thank you. I will try to return the favor.

The following entry came out of a discussion as to whether people who are published writers can be said to be better writers than people who have not. The short answer is "no," but the short answer is also incomplete. Funny how short answers are often that way. —JS

WHAT PUBLISHING IS

(March 18, 2005)

As there has been recent confusion on the matter, let's talk about what publishing is. Ready? Here it is:

Publishing is an engine for the production of competent writing.

That's it.

Now the details:

What is competent writing? Competent writing is writing that efficiently describes ideas and concepts to an audience, using a grammar that the audience can understand.

Why is publishing an engine for the production of competent writing? Because competent writing has a competitive advantage over incompetent writing. The book that competently describes the major battles of World War II, or a sex scene, or how to build and stain a backyard deck, has a distinct informational (and commercial) advantage over books with the same subjects that transmit their ideas poorly.

How does publishing select for competence? By employing competence-enhancing mechanisms at every step of writing production. The submission process exists (among other things) to weed out the grossly incompetent writing. The editing process exists to strengthen the text and to make sure its ideas are more easily assimilated by the reader. The design process aims to provide the text with a visual grammar that assists the goals of the text. The marketing process aims to promote the book's competence or (in the worst case scenario) minimize its competence failures.

What does this mean for writers? In a broad sense: If you are professionally published by a legitimate publisher, you are *probably* at the very least a minimally competent writer.

Points to make here:

1. Competent is *not* the same as good. "Good" is about taste and style; "competent" is about facility with the writing grammar of a language. Moreover, not every bit of competent writing needs to be "good"—you don't necessarily want a user manual to knock you on your ass with its prose style, you just want it to tell you how to use your damn toaster. With literature and non-fiction, there are any number of competent writers one might subjectively label "bad" writers—for all their ability to construct a sentence, the sentences they construct simply don't do anything for you.

Although competent is not the same as good, it's also the case that good books are always competent; at the very least, I've never heard of a good book that was also incompetently written (if you have, please enlighten me). Conversely, although it's possible for a competent book to be stylistically bad, *all* incompetent books are also bad (again, I'd be pleased to know of exceptions).

1a. Competent is not always, but can sometimes be, the enemy of "good." Adventurous or challenging writing often skates on the edge of accepted rubrics of competence, as writers try new forms (example: James Joyce's *Ulysses* or Samuel Delaney's *Dhalgren*), and as such runs counter to publishing's conservative tendencies to publish such work. Commercial publishing in particular wants what sells. However, it's also possible that competence can aid "good," if the traditionally competent work it publishes buys a publisher enough commercial and critical head-room to attempt the occasional stab at weirdness (*Dhalgren* was indeed published by *someone*, after all). This is where the heavy curtain of monolithic "publishing" is pulled back to reveal editors with personal preferences and a drive to publish important work from time to time, and damn the sales.

2. Published work is a valid general metric for writing competence; however unpublished writing and writers are not necessarily incompetent. Incompetent writers tend to remain unpublished, but writing is often rejected for reasons *other* than competence: The submissions editor may have too many of that sort of writing in the dock, for example. And since new writers are continually debuting, it's axiomatic that they would possess writing competence while still in an unpublished state. By the same token, lots of "good" writers and writing struggle to get published (or are not published at all). Published authors should not assume they are *better* writers than unpublished ones, although they very probably have more insight into the publishing process as a professional endeavor.

3. The competence engine of publishing does not run perfectly (but it runs pretty well). Incompetent writers and writing *do* get published—not a significant percentage, but not so infrequently as to be entirely unnoticeable. The reasons for this range from incompetent editors (not a frequent occurrence in professional publishing, to be sure) to authors and/or celebrities whose fame is commercially significant enough that they are cut a measure of competence slack that is not available to the average schmoe writer—and even then any publisher worth its salt would try to impose some amount of competence on the work. Be that as it may, if Stephen King or John Grisham *really* wanted to (and to be clear, I don't suspect they do), they could probably whip up a book comprised entirely of reviews of their own intestinal emanations ("A Bear in the Woods: 25 Years of Squatlogging, 1979-2004"), and some publisher somewhere would be pleased to publish it. Most writers do not have that luxury, and I think we can all be thankful for that.

Most writers who wish to be published must demonstrate competence *every single time* they endeavor to be published, or they won't be published for very long. This is why the occasional grumbling one hears that the publishing industry is *really* all about who you know doesn't ring true to people who have been published. Publishing rather ruthlessly excises incompetent writers, and a legitimate publishing company that released incompetent work on a regular basis would find itself out of business pretty quickly.

Through effort and wile and the judicious use of knee pads, an incompetent writer probably could get published by a legitimate publisher—once. But considering all the effort it would take to make *that* happen, it would probably be simpler to learn how to be a competent writer. Which brings us to our last point:

4. Writing competence is a learnable skill—and therefore most people are capable of being competent writers. Writing competently isn't rocket science; it requires the knowledge of certain grammatical rules, which are less difficult than, say, calculus, followed by lots and lots and lots and lots and lots of writing practice. Yes, some writers are gifted by God or nature to be great writers and have that great ineffable thing that makes their writing *sing* without any effort at all. The odds that person is *you* are slim.

For everyone else, it's the learnable writing skills that will be the things that get you published—and to be clear, it wouldn't *hurt* the sky-blue miracle writers to work on the nuts and bolts of the writing process so when and if the muse takes a hike they have something to fall back on. As a *practical* matter, assume you'll need the writing training and practice, even if secretly in your heart you *know* God himself touched your quill. Think of it as a publishing career seat belt.

So that's what publishing is, and how it gets done.

What you need to know about this piece going in is that I've sold two novels by posting them on my Web site, and then having editors make unsolicited offers for them. I've also sold two non-fiction books the same way (including, uh, the one you're reading right now). I also know of a small number of other people who have done this as well. It would be easy to assume that I think publishing one's self online is a good thing for people to do. But my response to this is: Well, not exactly. Here's why. —JS

WHAT ONLINE WRITING IS GOOD FOR, 2005 EDITION

(October 16, 2005)

This line in a blog entry over at the TechRepublic site made me twitch a little:

Apparently, the trendy new way to get noticed by book publishers is to serialize your novel online and let the editors find you.

Well, okay, if one defines "trend" as this maneuver working for three speculative fiction authors over three years (actually two-and-a-half, as one of the authors noted was an odd-duck combination, in that portions of her novel were spotted online, and the physical manuscript of her novel was also rescued from the slush pile). Meanwhile, probably more than a thousand books were sold in the spec fic arena in the same timespan by the traditional method of submitting work for editorial consideration. If you're an aspiring first-time author, I would, you know, look at the odds involved before making a decision.

The author of the linked article does thankfully note the long odds involved:

> ...*every one of the authors discourages people from relying on the tactic as a way to get discovered (sound advice, by my analysis), but do recommend it as a way of getting your writing before an audience and working the kinks out.*

To be entirely honest about it, however, if you are going to take the time and effort to put your writing online, I think it's far *less* useful to put your fiction online than it is to spend some time creating an interesting blog and cultivating an audience for it. This is not an "either/or" situation, of course, as I have done both. But I will say that one of these you should do first, and that's to work on your blog.

The reason why should be reasonably obvious if you look at your blog in strict marketing terms (which you *shouldn't* do in real life, because no one likes reading a site that is obviously tacked up for marketing purposes. I'll get to that later). Blogs are fabulous marketing tools because what they're good for is getting people involved with you as a writer; they're tuning in to read what's going on in your head and in your life, and to a very real extent are sharing your life with you. They commiserate when you suffer a setback, and congratulate when you get ahead, and otherwise view you as part of their circle of acquaintances—not just some writer, but someone they know and (provided you have comments and/or answer e-mail) interact with. In other words, at some point some percentage of them stop being merely readers and become fans.

Fans—and again, we're talking in strict marketing terms—are useful. They're useful because they're likely to be proactive not only in buying any non-blog-related writing output you might create, but because they'll also help you sell your work to others, just like fans of other creative people help those folks as well. They (probably) won't be able to help you sell a book to a publisher, but once you sell the book, they can be there to help give the book a decent send-off. That in turn will be useful to your publisher.

Indeed, I think as more time goes on, more and more publishers will be looking at first-time authors and asking what sort of "fandom" they already have. If I were an editor and I was presented with two first-time authors, one of whom was not online, and another who was and had a couple thousand people visiting their blog on a daily basis, all other things being equal, I'd go with the writer who is already online. That's a couple thousand people I don't have to introduce this writer to, and possibly a couple thousand people who can help me sell that writer as an author. First-time author unit sales are usually low enough that a couple thousand blog readers can make a real and significant impact on a first time author's sell numbers.

I don't expect such considerations will trump competent writing—given the choice between an exquisitely-written novel by a nobody and a crap novel by someone with a popular blog, I would hope an editor and publisher would decide the exquisitely-writing author was worth cultivating. But when the two writers are of equal competence, why *wouldn't* an editor go for the one that brings readers to the party? I certainly know the relatively large readership of the Whatever is a selling point in my publishers' eyes.

Having said all that, I think it's also true that the moment you start treating your site readership like monkeys to be marketed to, you run the very real risk of losing them. I think one's readers are happy to celebrate one's achievements, but they know the difference between you celebrating *with* them, and you marketing *to* them. Not every reader wants to be treated as a consumer, and this is even more of the case in the online world. If you're a writer and you've spent the time cultivating a relationship with people (and they with you), they're going to feel betrayed if the tone of your site devolves purely to "and here's *another* thing of mine to buy!" I don't think people mind when an author says such things—authors write books with the hopes of selling them, and most people get that—as long as it's not the *only* thing an author says. Such things need to be part of the conversational and narrative flow of a blog or journal, not a disjointed break from it.

To hammer this point one final time: Yes, a blog is a great way to market yourself. And the minute you think of your blog *primarily* in marketing terms is the minute you kill its usefulness. People aren't coming to your site to be marketed to; they're coming to be entertained and to catch up with you. Be real, or you're going to lose them.

Now, if you *do* want to post creative work online, I strongly suspect it helps to have already been engaged in the online world in other ways. I posted *Old Man's War* on the Whatever after I'd been online for more than four years; by that time I had a couple thousand people a day coming by to see what I was up to. The reaction to *OMW* was stronger and more immediate than the reaction to *Agent to the Stars*, which I posted in March of 1999, when I only had a couple hundred people visiting every day (see what I mean about it taking time to cultivate an audience?). No matter how you slice it, if you want whatever fiction you post online to be appreciated and noticed, you need to develop an online presence first.

If you don't want to bother generating an online presence before posting creative work online, here are some of the problems you can expect: Posting creative writing out of the blue just means you have this big mass of verbiage online; no one knows its provenance, which means they're less willing to take the time with it, because, after all, who are you? Creative writing is also more difficult to produce on a constant basis (particularly if you're aiming for quality), meaning that you can't update on a daily or near-daily basis, which is the most desirable frequency for writing online. Finally, creative writing is something akin to a performance, while blog writing is closer to a conversation. By and large I've found people want to talk back when they're reading online.

Upshot here: If you expect simply posting creative stuff online is going to open doors, you're probably delusional. It takes time—lots of time.

The good news is that it's now easier to develop an online presence than it was before. There are more options to do it simply, and the communities are significantly more developed (particularly in places like LiveJournal and AOL Journals (nb: I work for the latter)). There are also indeed a number of editors and agents online, particularly those focused in genres like SF/F, horror and romance, so it's not entirely inconceivable that you might get to know them and they might see your writing. You might even be asked to send in some writing, even if you haven't put your fiction online (ask fantasy author Jo Walton about that: her online posts were impressive enough that an editor asked if she'd ever considered writing fiction). But the real advantage will be that people get to know you, and get to like what you have to say. And that might have useful carryover into the rest of your writing life.

Can you *plan* on it? No. But you can *work* with it, if it does happen. And in the meantime, you might just simply enjoy writing online, which is a reward in itself.

WRITING TIPS FOR NON-WRITERS WHO DON'T WANT TO WORK AT WRITING

(February 12, 2006)

A writing question:

> *What writing tips would you whisper to those who aren't aspiring professionals, but would like to write better? If I asked you about losing weight and you said* "Diet and Exercise" *you'd be a) correct and b) ignored. So no ideas that take work. We want the quick fix! Tips like* "Edit your work" *aren't useful.* "Gerunds are your friend" *are.*

So, the task here: Tell y'all how to write better without you actually having to make an effort. Fine. Here's how I would do it.

(NB: These work pretty well for people who *do* want to be pro writers, too.)

0. Speak what you write: This is rule zero because all other rules follow on this. Basically: If what you're writing is hard to speak, what makes you think it's going to be easy to read? It won't be. So speak out loud what you write. If you can't speak it naturally, rewrite it. Simple.

1. Punctuate, damn you: For God's sake, is it *really* so hard to know where to put a comma? When people read, even in their brains, there's usually some part of them that is sounding out the words. Without appropriate punctuation, especially commas, that word-speaking part will eventually choke on the sentence. Having said that, there's a tendency to over-punctuate as well, particularly with exclamation points. Too little punctuation makes it seem you want to collapse someone's lung, too much makes it look like you're a 14-year-old girl writing an IM. You want to avoid both.

Here's a quick and dirty guide on when to use punctuation:

Periods: When you're writing down a thought and you're at the end of that thought, put a period.

Commas: When you're writing down a thought and you want to take a breath, whether mental or physical, put in a comma.

Semi-colon: Put these in your writing in the place where, in conversation, you'd arch your eyebrow or make some other sort of physical gesture signalling that you want to emphasize a point.

Colon: Use when you want to make an example of something: For example, just like this.

Question Mark: Quite obviously, when you have a question.

Exclamation point: When you're really excited about something. You almost never need to use more than one in a paragraph. Use more than one in a sentence and you damn well better be using it for humorous and/or ironic effect.

Dashes: You can use these when you've already used a colon or a semi-colon in a sentence, but be aware that if you have more than one colon or semi-colon in a sentence, you're probably doing something wrong.

Somewhat related: Use capitals when you should (beginning of sentences, proper nouns), don't use them when you shouldn't (pretty much every other time). Lots of people think not using capitals makes them look arty and cool, but generally it just makes the rest of us wonder if you've not yet figured out the magical invention known as the shift key. Alternately, the random appearance of capitals in inappropriate places makes us wonder if you don't secretly wish the Germans won World War II (and even the Germans are cracking down on wanton capitalization these days, so there you are).

2. With sentences, shorter is better than longer: If a sentence you're writing is longer than it would be comfortable to speak, it's probably too long. Cut it up. This is one I'm guilty of ignoring; I tend to use semi-colons when I should be using periods. In fact, I'd say the largest single editing task I have after writing a piece is to go in and turn semi-coloned sentences into two sentences (or more, God forgive me).

Shorter is also better with paragraphs, but there's such a thing as too short—take a look at a not-particularly-well-edited newspaper and you'll see a lot of single-sentence paragraphs, generally preceded or followed by other single-sentence paragraphs that should have been compressed into one paragraph. Good rule: one extended idea or discrete event per paragraph.

3. Learn to friggin' spell: I'm not talking typos here, because everyone makes them, and I make more than most. I mean genuine "gosh I really don't know how this is spelled" mistakes. This is particularly the case with basic spelling errors like using "your" when you're supposed to be using "you're" or "its" for "it's" (or in both cases, vice-versa). Here's a good rule of thumb: For every spelling error you make, your apparent IQ drops by 5 points. For every "there, they're, their" type of mistake you make, your apparent IQ drops by 10 points. Sorry about that, but there it is.

What's truly appalling is that even people with advanced degrees (I'm looking at you, scientists) screw these particular pooches. I look at some of the writing I see from people with MAs and PhDs after their names and I think *no wonder China's poised to kick our ass.*

Look, spelling isn't *hard.* Nearly every single computerized writing tool has a built-in spellcheck that will catch 90% of your spelling errors, and as for the rest of them, well, it isn't too much to ask adults to know the difference between "their" and "there." It's really *not.*

Also, here's a handy tip for those of you with Internet access (which, by definition, would be all of you reading this on my site). If you have a word, the spelling of which you're not sure, and you don't have a dictionary handy (either bound or online), copy the word, paste it into Google's search engine, and hit "search." If you've spelled it incorrectly, chances are really excellent that when your search results come up, up at the top Google will ask "Did you mean:"

and present whatever word it is that you're failing to spell. There's no shame in doing this.

Bottom line: Typos aside, there's no reason not to spell things correctly (and you really should get on those typos, too, although I note that I'm the last person in the world to ride folks on *that* one).

Related to this:

4. Don't use words you don't really know: It's nice to use impressive words from time to time, but if you use an impressive word incorrectly, everyone who *does* know what the word means will think of you as a pathetic, insecure dork. I'm just saying. Bear in mind that this is not limited only to "impressive" Latinate words, but also (indeed especially) to slang. Use slang incorrectly—or even use last year's word—and you'll look like *teh 1am3r*. Unless you're using the slang ironically, in which case you might be able to get away with it.

But generally: stick to words you *know* you know, or make real good friends with that there dictionary thingie.

5. Grammar matters, but not as much as anal grammar Nazis think it does: The problem with grammar is that here in the US at least, schools do such a horrible job of teaching the subject that most people are entirely out to sea regarding correct usage. It's the calculus of liberal arts subjects. But grammar need not be stupendously complicated; in the final reduction the point of grammar is to make the language clear to as many people as possible. Frankly, I think if most non-writers can manage to get agreement between their verb and their subject, I'm willing to spot them the whole "who/whom" conundrum.

Now, obviously, you *should* know as much grammar as you can; the more grammar you know, the better you can write. But the bottom line is just this: *Be as clear as possible.* If you're not confident about the grammar of a sentence, re-write it and strive for clarity. Yes, it's possible that in doing so the resulting sentence will lack *style* or something. But it's better to be plain and understood than to have people admire your style and have not the slightest idea what you're trying to say.

6. Front-load your point: If you make people wade through seven paragraphs of unrelated anecdotes before you get to what you're really trying to say, you've lost. Yes, Mark Twain and Garrison Keillor pull that stunt all the time. But: Surprise! You're not them. Also, there were lots of times when Twain just needed to get to the goddamn *point*, already.

Now, sometimes people write to find out *what* their point is; I think that's fine because I do that myself. But most of the time after I've figured out my point, I'll go back and re-write. Because that's the magic of writing: You can do that. It's not actually a live medium. No, not even in IM, since you can still re-write before you hit "send."

This point is more flexible than some of the others; sometimes you want to go the long way around to make your point because doing so makes the point stronger. However, *most* of the time it's better to let people know what you're doing than not, if only because then you have a better chance of them sticking around until the end.

7. Try to write well every single time you write: I have friends who I know can write well who send me the most *awful* e-mail and IMs because they figure it doesn't matter how many rules of grammar and spelling they stomp on because it's just e-mail and IM. But if you actually *want* to be a better writer, you have to be a better writer every time you write. It won't *kill* you to write a complete sentence in IM or e-mail, you know. The more you do it, the better you'll get at it until it will actually be more *difficult* to write poorly in e-mail and IM than not (mobile text messaging I understand has more limitations. But I tend to look at text messaging as the 21st Century equivalent of semaphore, which is to say, specialized communication for specialized goals).

There really is no excuse for writing poorly in one's blog. At least with IMs and e-mail your terrifying disembowelment of the language is limited to one observer. But in your blog, you'll look stupid for the whole world to see, and it will be archived for as long as humanity remembers how to produce electricity. Maybe you don't think anyone who reads your blog will care. But *I* read your blog—yes indeed I do—and I care. Madly. Truly. Deeply.

8. Read people who write well: Don't just read for entertainment, but also look to see how they do their writing—how they craft sentences, use punctuation, break their prose into paragraphs, and so on. Doing so takes no more time than reading what they write *anyway*, and that's something you're doing already. If you can see what they're doing, you can try to do it too. You probably won't be able to re-create their *style*, since that's something about that particular person. But what you can do is recreate their *mechanics*. Don't worry that your own "voice" will get lost. Be readable *first* and your own style will come later, when you're comfortable with the nuts and bolts of writing.

9. When in doubt, simplify: Worried you're not using the right words? Use simpler words. Worried that your sentence isn't clear? Make a simpler sentence. Worried that people won't see your point? Make your point simpler. Nearly every writing problem you have can be solved by making things simpler.

This should be obvious, but people don't like hearing it because there's the assumption that simple = stupid. But it's not true; indeed, I find from personal experience that the stupidest writers are the ones whose writing is positively *baroque* in form. All that compensating, you know. Besides, I'm not telling you to boil everything down to "see spot run" simplicity. I am telling you to make it so people can *get* what you're trying to say.

Ultimately, people write to be understood (excepting Gertrude Stein and Tristan Tzara, who were intentionally being difficult). Most people are, in fact, capable of understanding. Therefore, if you can't make people understand what you write, most of the time it's *not* just because the world is filled with morons, it's also because *you* are not being clear. Downshift. People will be happy to know what you're saying.

10. Speak what you write: Yes, I've covered this before. But now after all the other tips you can see *why* this makes sense. If you can't make your writing understandable to you, you can't make it understandable to others.

And now I'm off to speak this to myself. If I can do it with my writing, you can do it with yours.

~ᴡᴡᴡ~ Chapter Two: ~ᴡᴡᴡ~

YO HO, YO HO, A WRITER'S LIFE FOR ME

T his chapter is mostly about money. Oh, it's a *little* bit about me and how I got into writing and what some of the day-to-day experience of being a writer is like, and all that huggy, affirmative crap. But *mostly*, it's about money.

The reason for that is fairly simple: Writing is what I do for a living. This is how I pay my bills, buy my toys, heat my house, get gifts for my kid and also (and not incidentally) eat. I love to write, and I would do it even if I didn't get paid. But as long as I *can* get paid, I'm going to maintain a good focus on that aspect of my writing career. It keeps me from asking people if they want fries with that.

Now, this is the part of the intro where I'm supposed to tell you that we're living in an interesting time for writers, what with the imminent popular arrival of e-books and what have you, and all the challenges they will entail for writers, particularly ones who want to make money, but you know what? *Eh.* I've been waiting for the imminent popular arrival of e-books for about a decade now, and it seems to me that, one, books aren't very much like music or movies and maybe we'll be waiting for the imminent popular arrival of e-books for *another* ten years or so, and two, it's never *not* an interesting time for writers. Before the possibility of e-books and electronic piracy, writers had to worry about the rise of the chain book store and the decline of the supermarket book racks. Before that there was the initial consolidation of publishers into media megacorporations. And before that, there was, oh, I don't know, editors experiencing demonic possessions and devouring lagging midlist writers. It's always *something*.

I've been a professional writer for fifteen years, which is not enough time for a grand historical perspective on the profession, but *is* certainly enough time to know that you *can* make a living as a writer today—and a good living at that, if you work at it. The pieces in this chapter reflect some of the reality of being a working writer today. The things you read here might not have been true fifteen or twenty years ago; they might not be true fifteen or twenty years from now. But they are true now, and *now* is when I have to work as a writer.

Ready?

Because I said that this chapter would be about money,
let's not beat around the bush...

THE MONEY ENTRY

(March 14, 2006)

An e-mail this morning:

> *You've said before that you make more than most*
> *other writers. If you don't mind me asking, how*
> *much do you make? How do you know it's more than*
> *what other writers make?*

Just in case any of you were wondering whether people feel like they can ask me anything.

On the other hand, I have in fact suggested that I tend to make more money than other writers at my (low) level of notoriety, and I've talked dollar sums on convention panels where I've spoken about making money as a writer, so I don't suppose there's any reason not to talk about it here. And as it happens Krissy tallied up my 2005 income last week while preparing our taxes.

So: In 2005, from writing and editing, I made $100,600. And as it happens that is pretty much dead-on average for my writing income since 1998, which is the year I became a freelance writer. Some years I make more (the top year was

2001, when I made about $150,000 due to a huge amount of corporate work) and some years I make less (in 2004 I made about $80,000), but put it all in the pot and 100K is more or less where it averages out. This is my writing/editing income solely; our household income (which includes Krissy's salary, rental income and other income sources) is naturally higher, and you'll forgive me if I don't break that out for you because while I've talked about my writing income before, the rest of it is not for public consumption. Regardless, we're doing okay.

Where does this writing income come from? In roughly the order of percentage of income, thusly:

1. Corporate work: Work I do for various business clients, primarily in the financial and online sectors. I work with some of these folks directly and also work as a sub-contractor for marketing and consulting firms. This is the stuff I consider my "day job," in that it is consistent, to the extent that any freelance work can be, and therefore I can reliably budget this income (or more accurately, Krissy can, since she handles the finances in the Scalzi household). This is the stuff that pays the bills (my AOL blogging income is in this section).

2. Book income: This is primarily income from book advances, although last year for the first time I had income from royalties (on *Book of the Dumb* and *The Rough Guide to the Universe*) and also from foreign sales. Aside from the books that carry my name, this also includes contributions to the Uncle John's Bathroom Readers, in which contributors get an acknowledgment but not a byline. They pay well enough (and writing the stuff is fun enough) that I couldn't possibly care if my name is on every piece I write for them.

3. Magazine/Newspaper income: This is primarily from two sources: *The Official US PlayStation Magazine*, for which I write DVD reviews and commentary columns, and the *Dayton Daily News*, for which I write a separate DVD column and occasional features and columns. I will also occasionally sell a Whatever as a reprint to newspapers; two examples of this are the "Standing Up For Dubya" entry, which I sold to the *Philadelphia City Paper*, and the "Being Poor" piece, which was in the *Chicago Tribune* and other papers (although, as it happens, I chose not to take payment for that particular piece, which is not a usual thing for me). The OPM and DDN income is also predictible (I've been writing for both for a number of years), so this also gets put into the "money to pay bills with" planning ledger. For 2005, this amount also included income I got from guest-editing *Subterranean* magazine.

4. Short Fiction income: This is a new addition, based on the chapbooks I wrote for Subterranean last year ("Sketches of Daily Life" and "Questions for a Soldier"), for which I was paid pretty well (which is to say, higher than the general rate for SF short fiction). Be that as it may, short fiction is, by a significant divisible, the smallest section of my income. I don't tend to do much short fiction purely for economic reasons—my experience with Subterranean notwithstanding, I can be paid significantly more for writing short non-fiction than short fiction, and there are more places and opportunities to write short non-fiction. So that's what I gravitate to. Now, I do intend to write somewhat more short fiction in the near future (it's a form I want to get better at), but given the generally very low rates the field pays, I don't ever expect it to be a significant part of my income.

Generally speaking, there are four reasons I am able to pull down low six figures from writing on a regular basis. First, I am a reasonably competent writer who is reasonably easy to work with; I make it part of my writing ethic not to be a pain in the ass to clients and editors, and also to do what I can to give them what they want and need the first time. This is particularly the case in corporate work; my ego there is focused on hitting the clients' needs (it helps I have other outlets where I can do what I want when I want to). But all the way around I try to be useful and not a problem for the people I work with.

Second, which is an extension of the first, I have a lot of contacts in various writing spheres and an extensive writing history, which makes it easy for people to hire me/buy my work, because they can see what I've done before and know I can hit the marks that need to be hit. Third (and again, an extension of the first two), I have multiple writing competencies, so when work in one sphere is slow, I can work in another sphere of writing. This also allows me to develop additional competencies while still pulling down income in things I already have a track record in.

Finally: I write a *lot*. An average week will see me writing 20k-30k words across the various writing jobs I have (and at the Whatever, which does not generate income directly but which has significant indirect benefits). That's a million words a year, most of it pay copy. It adds up.

(Oh, one other thing: I'm also selective, which means I don't write everything that's offered to me; I have to see whether the job is actually worth my time relative to other opportunities that exist. This can lead to some painful choices; last year I turned down an opportunity to do what would have been a really fun book because I couldn't make it fit with other things I wanted and needed to do. I've also passed on work simply because there wasn't enough money there to make it worth my while. Turning work away is still painful—the paranoid voice in my head who says *you'll never work again* shouts the loudest at these times—but it's eventually necessary.)

I think it's possible that any competent writer who is not a pain in the ass to work with can pull down a reasonable sum of money working as a freelance writer, but I will also note that my ability to make a lot of money as a freelancer from my first year is non-typical and a little deceptive. I didn't begin as a freelance writer without experience; by the time I went freelance I had done a seven-year writing apprenticeship inside the confines of corporate America, first as a newspaper writer and then as a writer and editor at AOL. Both of these were extremely useful—the newspaper for writing quickly and to specification, and AOL for both corporate world experience and because AOL was a hothouse for ambitious folks who went out in the world to their own start-ups and called on me when they needed work done because they remembered who I was. So a lot of the years in which I *should* have been a starving freelancer, building up my chops, I was toiling happily for The Man and doing my chop-building there. Also, I was lucky in that the people I worked with were both ambitious and happy to get in touch with me for work. I have never been shy in admitting that luck has had a lot to do with my career; here's another example. Of course, luck only gets one so far; sooner than later I had to back up the luck with competence. Even so, it'd be disingenuous to suggest it was *all* me.

My experience is why among other things I tell people not to be in an all-fired rush to give up their day jobs. My time in corporate America allowed me to build a portfolio of skills that were useful when I went (somewhat unwillingly) into the freelance world; other people can and should do the same. Now, my corporate experience was directly on point to writing, which was additionally helpful, but even those folks with day jobs that are not directly related to writing still can get advantages from them while they are also working on their writing. And of course, all this comes in handy whether one intends to make writing one's primary revenue source or not.

Let me note two obvious things. First, writing income is not necessarily an indicator of how good a writer is stylistically. Speaking personally I can think of several writers who I think write better than I, who make less than I do—and several who I think write worse, who make more. Second, writing income isn't necessarily an indicator of writing happiness. Some writers don't care all that much about money and write either for fun or because they feel compelled to; using writing income as a metric for them isn't very useful or relevant. As for me, I think it's possible I could make more as a writer than I do, but at this point in time it would mean taking on more work I have no interest in, which wouldn't make me very happy.

What writing income corresponds to is competence, opportunity and willingness. I am a competent writer; I am fortunate to have a lot of opportunities to sell work and I'm willing to do a lot of work, including some stuff which isn't particularly exciting in the "writers are so bohemian" sense. Commensurately I make a fair amount of money doing writing. Most writers have these three factors in varying amounts and make corresponding amounts of money. There are other factors to be sure; these are the three big ones, however.

Naturally, I'm happy with what I make, and I think overall I have a good balance of work that's fun and interesting, and work I'm happy to do because it gives me a stable income base for my life and my family's needs (and when those two factors overlap, as they sometimes do, even better). I wouldn't mind making more, although not at the expense of my current quality of life in terms of family time and range of projects. I don't mind making less, as long as my family's needs are met and the work I get to do is sufficiently appealing for its own sake. Writing is a business for me, and also a calling. The key is being able to get to a happy medium between those two axes. Where that medium is, work and income-wise, is different for everyone. I think you find it out mostly by doing.

15 THINGS
ABOUT ME
AND BOOKS

(December 11, 2005)

1. I don't remember not being able to read. Or more accurately, one of the very first memories I am sure about was reading *One Fish, Two Fish, Red Fish, Blue Fish*. I was about two at the time.

2. Possibly the most influential book in my life was *The People's Almanac*, which I encountered when I was six, at my grandmother's house. It seemed that everything in the world it was possible to know was contained in that book. So naturally I was astounded a few years later when *The People's Almanac #2* showed up.

3. When I was in kindergarten my teachers had me tutor third graders on reading. As you may expect, the third graders weren't pleased about that.

4. My love affair with astronomy started in kindergarten as well; I can still see the book on astronomy with pictures of stars of all different hues, and their temperatures listed beneath.

5. My mother used to scrounge old Time-Life science books and science textbooks for me from thrift stores. That was the coolest thing ever.

6. The first science fiction novel I'm entirely sure of reading was *Farmer in the Sky* by Robert Heinlein. The first fantasy novel I'm entirely sure of reading is *The Dark is Rising* by Susan Cooper.

I'm pretty sure I also read *A Wrinkle in Time* around the same time, but I'm not sure whether it came before or after those other two books.

7. Because I both grew up poor and was in awe of books, to this day I read my paperbacks in such a way that I don't crack the spine. If you were to come over to my house, it would appear that all the paperbacks have never been open. They have, trust me.

8. In high school, I burned one of my math textbooks at the end of the year and immediately regretted having done so, to the point of actual shame. I still have the remains of the book to remind me that was essentially a betrayal of my beliefs.

9. It's only in the last few years that I've regularly bought hardcover books.

10. You would think that one of the cool things about being a writer is I can go into a bookstore and see my own books there, and you'd be right. But what's even cooler is going into a bookstore and seeing my *friends'* books there. It's like being able to visit them wherever they are.

11. There are some books in which I enjoy the writing so much, I can't bring myself to finish the book, because that would mean there is no more of the writing to read.

12. I am delighted that my daughter Athena both thinks that going to the bookstore is a treat, and that not being able to buy the entire bookstore is a tragedy.

13. As much as I love books, I am not a serious collector. I don't particularly care about first editions and the like. The value of books is what's inside them.

14. With the exception of Twain, I don't like reading novels written before the 1920s. The writing style is so different that it's distracting.

15. I'm not an audio book person. I understand why

there is a market for them, and I don't think ill of people who listen to them—that's just silly. And I wouldn't mind if one of my novels were made into an audio book. But, really, they're not for me. I read with my eyes, not my ears. That said, if someone were ever to do an audiobook version of one of my books, I would be very interested to hear it—it would be interesting to hear the sound of my literary voice.

15 THINGS
ABOUT ME
AND WRITING

(December 11, 2005)

1. The first time anyone told me specifically that I could write and should keep working at it was when I was in the sixth grade; it was my teacher, Mr. Johnson. His comments were amplified by my freshman composition teacher, Mr. Hayes.

2. Since freshman year in high school, I've never considered doing anything else with my life *other* than being a writer.

3. At the risk of sounding egotistical, in a general sense writing is *very* easy for me. Specific projects may be difficult due to research or other factors, but the actual sitting down and crafting the words has never been a problem. When other writers talk about how hard writing is for them I can sympathize but not really empathize.

4. Despite it being easy to do, I can get distracted from writing pretty easily, which can get me in trouble. To some extent this is mitigated by my being able to write quickly (5K words a day is not uncommon for me), but one thing I continually try to work on is my ability to structure my time effectively.

5. I find it difficult to write if I'm not using a keyboard— the act of typing is definitely part of my writing process. I write very differently when I am writing long hand or if I am dictating, and (in my opinion) not better. For this reason I am a bit anal about my keyboards. When I bought my Mac, I knew within a week that I couldn't *think* using the keyboard that came with the Mac; I tossed it unceremoniously. Now both my Mac and my PC have Logitech keyboards. Logitech keyboards apparently help me think.

6. I'm not a writer who works well in group settings. I don't like workshops (I have a caveat to that coming up) and I prefer my relationships with other writers be casual rather than professional; I would much rather have a drink with a writer and talk shop than try to co-write or start some sort of writing group. Now, this does *not* mean I think writers who like collaboration and creative consultation with other writers are doing something *wrong*; if it works for them, that's good and well. I just don't have the inclination for that myself.

7. Having said that, here's the caveat: I think it would be fun to *teach* at a workshop, and I like being an editor (on occasion; I don't know if I have the temperament to do it full time). The fact that I'm interested in teaching and editing but *not* in peer review and collaboration speaks volumes about me, I'm sure, but as I don't think what it says about me is a bad thing, that's fine.

8. Like most writers, I have a hard time judging what writing of mine is going to be particularly resonant with readers (and editors). Some of the writing I thought was not my best has been my most successful; some of the writing I liked the most no one has noticed. What *is* important is that I know when I'm writing crap, and that writing almost never gets seen by anyone else. So while I can't tell which of my writing is going to be successful, I at least know all the writing I put out there meets a minimum standard of readability, and that minimum standard is fairly high.

9. And having said *that*, I do have to say that one of my great challenges as a writer is making sure that my writing is more than *merely* facile. Writing quickly and not having to struggle to write is a blessing, to be sure, in pounding out sale copy; however, it can present huge issues in quality control. I threw out the first chapter of *The Ghost Brigades* about six times because what I wrote was perfectly readable, but it wasn't *good*—and yes, there is a difference between "readable" and "good".

10. As a writer, I am not particularly interested in description unless it's necessary to the plot. For this reason, I think, I am sometimes asked if my novels started out as screenplays (the convention in screenplays at the moment is not to be overly specific in description, since being so limits the film's casting directors and production designers).

11. Speaking of which, I have yet to write a screenplay. I'm vaguely interested in the format and I suppose if someone wanted to pay to me try to do one, I would. But it's not a storytelling format that calls to my soul. Having said that, I think I would be a pretty good script *doctor*, and I think it would be a lot of fun trying to bang an already-existing script into shape.

12. I'm not in the slightest bit romantic about writing— I love doing it and I would do it even if it weren't my job, but as it happens it is my job, and since it's my job one of my aims is to make a lot of money doing it, so I don't have to do anything else. This is occasionally off-putting to other folks but I don't worry about that much. Being unromantic about writing doesn't make one a *hack*—that comes when you don't give a crap about what you write, just as long as you get paid. I want to get paid, but I care about what I write. I write for money, but I don't write *just* for money.

13. Every year I buy a Writer's Market, and every year I never use it. I buy it to remind myself that if everything I have going for me at the moment craters and collapses, I still have a couple thousand other chances to still keep writing professionally.

14. I have no good answer for "what would you do if you didn't write?" I can't imagine not writing. I can imagine not making a *living* at it, but that's an entirely separate thing. If I couldn't make a living writing, I don't think it would particularly matter what I did, since I doubt my self-image would be connected to that job.

15. I think I'm a good writer. I also think I've been a very lucky writer. Both have worked to my advantage at different times in my career. I know that some better writers have been less lucky than I, and that some worse writers have been more lucky. In both cases, I try not to worry too much about it. I just try to make sure that the luck I have eventually gets justified by good writing. If that gets me to a place where I can spread some of my luck around, so much the better.

And now, an expanded take on wanting to be a writer,
and how I got to that point. —JS

WANTING TO BE
A WRITER

(August 19, 2005)

Reader sxKitten asked:

When did you realize you wanted to be a writer,
and what motivated you to start writing seriously
(writing in hopes of being published as opposed to
writing just for fun)?

As for the "wanting to be a writer" thing, I think I've
mentioned before when it happened, but just in case I didn't,
here it is: I started thinking about being a writer about age
12, when it became clear I was good at it (good relative to
being 12, mind you) and also coincidentally it became clear
that I wasn't likely to become an astronomer (my first choice
of professions) because I did math only slightly better than
Clever Hans, and that wasn't going to be acceptable if I
wanted to be a truly *useful* astronomer. The confirmation
that I was going to be a writer came to me when I was 14,
when I was the only kid to get an "A" on a writing assignment
that the Freshman English composition teacher (John Hayes)

assigned to his classes, and I got it for a story that really didn't require all that much effort to write (and was fun to do as well). No stupid kid I, I made the connection: Writing = pretty easy; Everything else = more work than it's worth.

The matter of what my future profession would be was pretty much settled then, and I never really considered doing anything else as a profession after that. This was useful because unlike most people I didn't have to suffer through the existential angst of wondering what I was going to do with my life, with the commensurate academic and emotional casting about trying to figure out what fit. Indeed, as friends who knew me during my developmental years would no doubt tell you, I was actually fairly driven toward those things I thought would be useful in a writing career and rather deeply apathetic toward those things that were not.

This (combined with my own inherent laziness) was why I maintained a steady 2.8 GPA through high school and college; I would ace my "useful" classes and get Ds in the classes I didn't care about, because, really, I didn't *care*. This drove both my mother and my college girlfriend absolutely nuts for differing reasons, although I'm reasonably sure if you asked them about it now, they would grudgingly admit that in retrospect I knew what I was doing. *I'm* not entirely sure I would admit I knew what I was doing, and I suspect that if I had to do it over again, I would probably try harder in the classes in which I didn't try—not necessarily for the grades but because knowledge is useful, and wasting it because you don't think you need it is stupid. But life doesn't give you do-overs in that respect (although you can make it up in extra credit!), and in the end I was fortunate that my cavalier attitude toward my own education seems not to have caused any lasting damage.

As to the question regarding what motivated me to start writing "seriously"—well, after the age 14 revelation that writing was easy and fun and most other things weren't, I would suggest that I was writing "seriously" from that moment forward, since I made the decision to make writing my profession. Writing "seriously" should not be confused with writing professionally or even writing *well*—but I was aware that what I was writing was part of a continuum which would (hopefully) lead to a career in writing.

Now, I don't want to suggest that I had a huge amount of sagacity or perspective on the matter when I was young. Like many teens who are good at something to a degree that most of their friends and acquaintances aren't, I had a rather outsized opinion of my writing and its quality, a fact which leads me to recall a number of incidents involving me and my writing which cause me to cringe today. Indeed, allow me a moment to say the following:

To all the people the younger me forced my writing upon when you were merely being polite about my enthusiasms: So sorry. Really. It won't happen again.

I have friends from high school and college who haven't read much of anything I've written since those days because they had to suffer through what I wrote then, and I was also aggressive about making them suffer through it. As a result I am much more circumspect today about doing that sort of crap. This is not the same as saying I've entirely quelled the little needy "Look! Look! Aren't I so good and clever and funny *and don't you just love me?!?!?*" demon that I have, because, oh, it's *there*. And it's not entirely unuseful, especially when it transmutes into a capability to tirelessly work the publicity rounds. But I do try to keep it in its cage most of the time, and not spring it on people who are actually interested in me for things *other* than my writing, or are just being polite.

(Not entirely surprisingly, the Whatever is very useful for this, since it allows me a space to be my show-offy and sometimes appallingly arrogant self without having to take the commensurate step of forcing it on other people. After all, no one's putting a gun to people's heads and making them come to my site every day (as far as I know). It's exhibition without the pushy pushy pushy that gives exhibition that queasy edge. Yes, I want to be liked, and seen as a clever writer. But these days I don't want to be liked so much that I need to rub myself (or every little bit of my writing) on other people. My days of being literary frotteur are largely over.)

To go back to the point after this long, self-flagellating digression, whatever my earlier estimations of my writing abilities, most of what I wrote when I was younger was written with an eye for it being published and read by other people; I have almost no personal writing of any sort— what little there is exists in the form of high school and college-era poems and song lyrics. Otherwise, what unpublished material I have exists as failed book proposals. Of that stuff, I think it was almost all *fun*, otherwise I wouldn't have done it, but it's all also "serious." Generally speaking, I didn't distinguish between the two. Even the Whatever, which began as an uncommercial site (and still is, mostly), was also begun to keep in practice for commercial writing. And over time, I've sold quite a few things that were originally published here, and I'm aware how the site has helped my career by helping me build an audience. When I wrote *Agent* as a "practice" novel (i.e., for fun and not for profit), after I was done I put it up and offered it as shareware (i.e., for an audience, and for them to pay me if they liked it). And of course, I've sold it as a book since then. So you see that the line is very blurry between my "fun" and my "serious" when it comes to writing.

If anything, I'm somewhat less concerned as I get older about what's "fun" and what's "serious" in terms of writing. At this point in time, with seven books published and two more in the pipeline for 2006, reasonably good prospects for selling books after that point, and a solid career in writing outside of books, I'm very comfortable with who I am in a professional sense. I don't really feel I have to prove any more that I've "made it" as a writer or measure up to a particular standard. I have goals, of course, in terms of writing: I want to write things I like; I want to write things my publishers can sell; and when at all possible I'd like the two former statements to be well-integrated with each other so I can continue in this happy cycle until I croak.

I recognize that a number of writers—many excellent— make a strong distinction between their "serious" and "fun" work, or can register a point when their writing stopped being simply about the joy of expression and started angling toward something more cash and attention-generating, but I've never been that way. I'm not an Emily Dickinson type, either, content to write stuff and keep it in a drawer for the spiders and the executor of my estate. For better or worse, I've always written with an eye toward my writing being seen and (hopefully) enjoyed by as many people as the medium allows. What you see is what you get. An interesting question, which I can't answer, since I'm inside of it, is whether the notably "popular" tone of my writing comes initially from my own personal voice, or the narcissistic desire to reach a large audience. I *suspect* it's the former, but then I would.

Having now asked that question, I do wonder what I would write if I decided to write something that I *didn't* intend other people to see. To be honest, the idea is so alien to me, I'm having a hard time thinking of anything at all. Which is, of course, fascinating in itself. I'll have to think about it some more.

EXPIRED CONTRACTS

(August 6, 2001)

Last week, one of my writing contracts expired and was not renewed. Normally, this is an event that would fill me with a sort of indescribable dread. As a freelance writer, what little sense of security I have in life is in the form of the long-term contracts, usually of six months to a year in duration. These are the way I know that I'll have a house six months from now (not to mention will be able to, you know, feed my darling wife and child).

I think of these contracts as my actual "income," which is to say the money that goes to pay bills. The spot work I do each month my brain sort of considers as "free" money, with no initial assigned purpose, to be spent on frivolities or, on occasion, saved. This sounds sort of confusing, but what it really means is that as a practical matter, I live within the means provided me by my long-term contract income, not my *total* writing income. So you can see how losing some of that monthly long-term income could be a little nerve-wracking.

However, when I was told this particular contract would not be renewed, what I actually felt was…a tiny bit of relief. The contract had been something of a mismatch anyway; I could feel it, as could my client (with whom, I should note, I have other contracts, most of which are just fine). The extra income was of course nice, but there was also a small sense of aggravation that I had about the work, and some mis-communication on both ends about how the work was going and what needed to be done. Most of the rest of my long-term contract work is sort of fun, but this one wasn't as much so; it was more like actual work.

This is not to say that I wouldn't have taken the work if they had decided to renew. But I wasn't upset when they decided not to. The fact is, everyone deserves to have the work they feel fits their requirements, and this really wasn't on either side. I was fine with walking away. Or so I thought; I did an internal gut check, however, just to be sure. And really, no qualms.

This is actually a fairly important thing for me as a working writer. In the last year or so, I've reached a level of experience and income where I was pretty sure that losing a little work wouldn't bother me terribly much; I could take the financial hit and move on, and my writing experience would help me to replace the income in short order. But there's a difference between thinking that, and what one actually feels in real life when it happens. Having the real life verification is nice.

It also helped that around the same time this one client was telling me they would not renew, another client overnighted a year-long contract formalizing my relationship with them. So while one chunk of money was taken out of the "long-term income" ledger, another chunk, of more or less equal size, dropped in. Net, my long-term income is about the same. And I've added a couple of sources of spot income in the last couple of months, so I'm not working on a deficit there. Really, I've been worse.

I should note that my writing career is the only place in my life where my devoutly agnostic belief system is routinely challenged; my writing life has been (so far) pretty much a series of upgrades. And the timing is almost always weirdly appropriate, as it was in this case—one contract went away, and another, mostly better, pops up in its place. This has happened enough times in my career that it gets a little spooky, and it does make me wonder if someone actually might be up there, looking out for me. I would not be presumptuous enough to say it's God Him/Her/Itself—a being that flings galaxies at each other just to see how they will fly apart really has more important things to do than to pay attention to my career. But maybe a guardian angel. Who knows. All I know is that for whatever reason, I'm profoundly grateful my career has gone like it has. So just in case someone *is* paying attention up there: Thanks. Really. Very much.

There's a flip side, of course—time, time, always time; something needed and something in dangerously short supply. For example, on Mondays I usually write a newsletter, a Whatever and a video game review. Well, this week, the newsletter and the Whatever were written on Sunday, because on Monday I have to make a boatload of phone calls—first to finish the argin'-fargin' business article I was writing last week, and second to gather information on another article, which will be a cover story for a magazine—my first cover story ever, and I'm thrilled beyond words to be able to do it, presuming these people return my argin'-fargin' phone calls. These pieces are important enough that I can't have other work in my way. So (for now, at least), my work week has expanded ever-so-slightly, and now it's really time to see if I actually do have time management skills (I do. But like a reluctant gunfighter, I hate to whip 'em out unless I have no other choice).

The thing about the dropped contract is that really, for the first time, I can say *it's just business*—I'm not questioning my skills or my abilities, and I don't see the dropped contract as a referendum on my career. It's just work. Sometimes work comes, sometimes it goes, and sometimes it's not the worst thing that could happen when it goes. It's nice to be at this point. Let's see how long it lasts.

CRITICISM

(January 29, 2003)

A reader sent me an e-mail yesterday letting me know that while he enjoyed *Old Man's War*, he had a couple of suggestions about the story that he thought would make it even better, which he then proceeded to provide to me. It was basically all I could do to keep from chewing off the inside of my cheek.

It's not this guy's fault, mind you. I understand that he was genuinely trying to be helpful, and I appreciate that he liked the story enough to offer suggestions on how it could be improved. The intentions are good and I wouldn't want this guy to think I thought he was out of line for making suggestions, or that he should be stomped to death by 40-foot fighting robots for having the temerity to question my prose.

But having said that, "constructive criticism" drives me up a freakin' wall. To be entirely honest, I like criticism of my work to be generally unconstructive. I don't mind if, say, you tell me my dialogue stinks and is unrealistic, but I do mind if you tell me my dialogue stinks and the way to fix it is to do A or B or C. When I had *Old Man's War* out to beta testers, I asked them to catch grammar, spelling and continuity errors, and to tell me what they liked and didn't like about the story. But I also specifically told them not to offer suggestions on how to fix things. Why? Because I didn't want to hear them. It's enough for me to know if you think something's not working in the writing. It's my job as a writer to figure out how to fix these problems—or not, since something you might see as a bug in the writing is something that I might see as a feature.

Of course, this little quirk of my writing character comes across as arrogance, and I cop to that. I've always been arrogant when it comes to writing; I remember back as a first year student in college getting into trouble with my Art History TA when I refused to participate in classroom peer review of other students' papers. I refused on the grounds that inasmuch as the other students weren't actually qualified either as English or Art instructors, any comments they might have would be of questionable utility to me and therefore a waste of my time, and because if I was going to have review other people's work and basically do the TA's job, I wanted to get paid. This position assured me of getting reamed by the TA when it came time to get papers graded (I think I ended up getting a C- in the class), but I didn't care about that. And, irony of ironies, as soon as I'm done with this Whatever, I'll be starting an article on the Dada movement and getting paid nicely for it. So we can see how the battle of the C-minus-giving-TA vs. my youthful arrogance eventually panned out.

But aside from the question of my arrogance (or at least only tangentially related to it) comes the question of the critic's competence. Everyone's entitled to their own opinion, and speaking as a professional critic, I'm all for people expressing their point of view. You don't need to be a professional musician to know you like a particular piece of music, or a professional writer to know what you like and don't like about an article or story. Lots of creative people seem to think that only their peers are qualified to

criticize, but that's just a stupid defensive measure creative types pull out of their ass when they don't want to
admit that being criticized simultaneously stings and
deflates the ego.

While everyone's competent to express an opinion
about whether something works, it doesn't stand to reason
that everyone is in a position to suggest how the piece
might be improved. Independent of the specific critic,
there's no reason to believe that the piece would be
improved if, say, different plot branches were utilized, or if
certain motivations were explored, or whatever. The end
result of these changes could be a worse piece, or a better
one, or simply one that is equally bad in a completely different way. Changing something is not implicitly equivalent to improving something. Back around the *Murmur* era
of things for REM, people complained that they couldn't
understand Michael Stipe's lyrics. But if they could, would
the music have been better? Not necessarily; Stipe's mad-
dening mumble was part of early REM's allure. *Murmur*
might have been better if you could hear what Stipe was
saying; but then again, it might have been worse.

Then there's the matter of personal competence as it
relates to making suggestions about writing. No offense,
people, but most of you aren't professional writers or editors, and that does make a difference. When Patrick Nielsen
Hayden comes to me with specific suggestions about what
needs to be done to punch up *Old Man's War* (as he's
already told me he will), you're damn right I'll listen; he's
Senior Editor of Tor and in that capacity knows how to
shape text so that it's both successful creatively and has a
shot in the marketplace, and those are two things I want the
book to be and have. Were another working novelist to offer
unsolicited advice on a plot point, I would likewise listen

attentively. These people have the real world experience that convinces me they know what they're talking about.

Short of those categories, however, I'm liable to ask myself how much you know about the dynamics of writing professionally, and if the answer I get is "not much," I will then ask myself why I should be listening to your specific writing suggestions. Doctors don't listen to suggestions from their baker on how to perform surgery (or if they do to be polite, they don't usually take them very seriously). They listen to doctors. Likewise, when it comes to the nuts and bolts of writing, I go to writers and editors first. Yes, I realize this goes back to the whole "arrogance" thing. But, you know, look—I've been writing professionally for well over a decade now. This is what I do. Financially speaking, this is all I do. This *is* my day job. When it comes to writing, I'm pretty confident I know what I'm doing (most of the time).

I do try not to be stupid in my arrogance. When I was writing my astronomy book, I had a couple of friends with PhDs in astronomy look over some early chapters, on the principle that they, being doctors of astronomy, were eminently qualified to tell me if and when I had my head up my rectum (it wasn't, mostly). And I'm not saying that non-writers can't have excellent suggestions about the craft of writing; they can and do, both in a general sense and specifically relating to my work. I'm not even saying that I don't sometimes ask for advice from non-writers, or writers who are not yet professional writers; I've done both, and my writing is better for it.

What I am saying is that if you're not a writer or editor, and you offer me specific writing advice without prompting, you should know I'm going to consider the source in evaluating how useful the advice is to me. Please don't be too offended if my estimation of its utility ultimately differs from yours. I do appreciate the thought, honestly. But this isn't one of those situations where it's only the thought that counts.

GET ME
REWRITE

(February 20, 2004)

I've terrified my reader Tamar with a comment I made in a recent entry thread on the subject of rewriting, so it's worth clarifying. In the comment thread for the entry, John Popa asked: "As an aspiring-to-be-published writer, I'm curious as to how much rewriting you expect from this point? How 'done' is this 'done?'" My response, in part:

> *I rewrite only very rarely, mostly because I tend to resolve most of my writing issues during the initial writing. In some sense I think "re-writing" is an artifact of the days of typewriters, when it wasn't easy or practical to rework material on the fly. With computers, it's much simpler to makes changes as you go along.*

This strikes Tamar as very wrong. While granting me props for my mad writing skillz (which I appreciate), Tamar not unjustifiably worries that I'm setting a bad example by eschewing rewrites, noting on her personal site:

> *… it scares me to think of some writer out there taking his opinion to heart, someone like my friend, looking for validation and an outside justification to avoid the work that needs doing. The world already has too many bad, unedited novels.*

121

I would agree that there are indeed too many bad, unedited novels out there (and too many bad edited ones, too, although that's a different matter entirely), and I would also agree wholeheartedly that as a writer I'm probably a terrible example to follow. But *that* doesn't surprise me in the least; I've always figured that was the case. Mamas, don't let your babies grow up to be John Scalzi.

I also don't want to single myself out as a writer who is just *so* good I don't need to rewrite—I mean, I think I'm a pretty good writer, y'all, but off the top of my head I can think of quite a few I think are better than me. I have no idea what *their* philosophy on rewrite is. And it might be that after my editor reads the book, he'll ship it back to me with a note that reads "Are you *high?* This is crap!"—a possibility which I note is even *more* realistic now, since last night I was rereading the book and I suspect my copy edit forgot to correct the name of one character changing from "Bob" to "Bill" about two-thirds of the way through. As they say: D'oh!

Be that as it may, I don't do rewrites—or more accurately, I haven't *done* rewrites; I may do them in the future (never say never). Why haven't I done rewrites? Mostly because I never have, ever (there's an exception to this, which I will get to). Back in high school, I had a history teacher who would make us turn in our first drafts of papers along with our final drafts; I would write the paper and then write out a "first draft" outline based on what I'd written (suitably messed up so as to show "improvement" from the rough draft to the final). From this undoubtedly bad practice I've continued with a basic philosophy of things being done when I'm done writing them.

The only defense I can possibly offer for it is that it seems to work for me. My non-fiction books were sent in to editors as originally written, and were all generally well-regarded by the editors and reviewers (particularly the *Universe* book, which pleases me to no end). *Old Man's War*, which sold to Tor, was essentially the first version of itself as well; I made some minor changes based on comments from a cadre of trusted beta testers, but nothing that qualifies as a true rewrite. The first short story I wrote for sale sold as an original edition (and to the first place I submitted. Whoo-hoo!). And with articles both for magazines and books, editors tell me (usually) one of the reasons they like working with me is that I turn in copy they don't have to fiddle with all that much. That copy again tends to be the original text. In short, I have no *objection* to the concept of rewriting, I just haven't *had* to. What I do works for me so far.

(The exception to this: business writing, which is *constantly* rewritten to suit client needs, which are, more frequently than not, a moving, evolving and—one must say—capricious target. I can't tell you the number of times I'll finish something for a client, and they'll say, "Hey, this is great, but we're changing the focus—can you rewrite?" My response: I get paid for business writing by the hour. Of *course* I can rewrite.)

I attribute not having to do a lot of rewrite to several factors, which include:

• **Years working at a newspaper.** You learn to write fast and reasonably good and in a manner which does not require substantial editing. Or your editors and copyeditors stab you to death and hang your corpse in the newsroom as a warning to the other staff writers.

• **A relatively high personal crap detection system.** I am, thank God, not under the illusion that everything I write is pure gold. I write a *lot* of crap. I just don't (usually) let other people see it. Like every other writer in the universe I have several trash bags full of stories, articles and meanderings that were strangled the very instant I realized how hideously misshapen they were. I don't tend to spend any time trying to revive these creative abortions through rewriting; I tend to believe (and this is strictly as relates to my own writing) that rewriting these turds would merely end up with me having a highly polished turd on my hands. I don't mind producing turds, which are a natural and healthy part of life. I just don't want them to come out of my brain and through my fingertips.

• **A relatively realistic assessment of my strengths and weaknesses as a writer.** And complementary to that, a willingness to write to my strengths and distract people from my weaknesses through the use of hand gestures and shiny bits of foil while I work on those weaknesses offstage. This is not to say that I only write what I already know; that'd be stupid. But it means I'm generally happy to do things incrementally.

For my novel *The Android's Dream*, which I just completed, my big personal innovation is third-person storytelling and multiple storylines. Not a revolutionary advance in the genre of storytelling in general, but a useful and necessary step for me as a writer, and one I could take while still (hopefully) churning out a fun and readable story. I don't know what the next step for me will be yet, although I have a few ideas. But I'll guarantee that it'll be a relatively small advance and that if it works well you won't notice it because you're enjoying the story I've written. If I do enough of these in tandem, several books down the road I'll be a much better writer *and* hopefully will have built a following.

This does mean that there are things you won't see me do, at least for a while. One of the reasons I love China Mieville's writing, for example, is that it's a style I simply cannot do. It doesn't mean his style is inherently better or worse than mine (although I cheerfully allow at this juncture that of the two of us he is the better writer), merely that I can't do it. Perhaps after a few more books are under my belt, I can try something along that line. We'll have to see.

• **A stint as an editor.** Which did two things for me: First, it made me appreciate the pain editors go through on a daily basis, and the pain I personally made them go through with some of my writing, thus forever after prompting me to respect the work they do for writers and to see them as a partner in the process rather than an enemy—and also to try to get them material they could work with (i.e., it added a significant boost to my personal crap detector). Second, it made me rather more aware of what works in writing and why—both in a general sense, and in the sense of my own personal tastes and inclinations.

I *don't* say this makes me a fabulous editor of my own work; like any writer, I'm really close to what comes out of my head. I *do* say it makes me more sensitive to what's working and what's not *as* I write. Once you've wrenched your head into an editorial mindset, it stays with you, and that's a damn useful thing. I will note that I think it is *incredibly* significant that I only started selling books after I spent time being an editor. Related to this:

• **Years as a critic.** I've spent countless hours watching and reading storytelling and then writing about how and why it works—or doesn't. Most of this has involved movies, which I think has definitely rubbed off on my writing;

when my fiction agent first read my work, he asked me if I had originally envisioned them as movies. The answer was no, but I could see why he thought that. If you spend a significant portion of your life looking at storytelling and having to make an opinion on it—and then having to *explain* that opinion to an audience—then you learn about structure and story and what works and what doesn't (or at least what works and what doesn't for *you*).

As an aside, I find that being a critic has also given me a tremendous confidence to write the stuff I know I like as a reader. As a critic, I'm not tremendously impressed with writing (or movies or music) that is intentionally opaque or difficult or obscure—none of which is necessarily a synonym for "challenging," which good art often strives to be—and I also see the value in entertaining an audience for the simple sake of entertaining an audience (especially when I personally am entertained). So paradoxically, I think being a critic has made me less of a snob. This is good for me as a writer, because my novels are not, shall we say, high-fiber brain food at this point. I want them to be entertaining because *I* like to be entertained. I'm writing the books I'd want to read when I'm stuck in some airport hell, with a flight cancelled and nothing to do until they call my name for standby.

• **Doing a buttload of rewrite in my head.** I take marathon showers—we're talking 45 minutes to an hour—not because I'm a filthy, filthy man (or not *just* because) but because I tend to get my best thinking done there. And why not? I mean, you're just *standing* there. Why *not* think?

And what I tend to think about is: *How the hell am I going to get myself out of the corner I've just written myself into?* I spend a lot of time just standing there, going through plot scenarios in my head, chopping off story ideas that aren't working, pumping up the ideas that are working and generally wrestling with a lot of the issues that I suspect other writers deal with on the written page. Much of this thinking relates to immediate writing issues, but I also use the time to think up big ideas and then let them accrete in my brain—stuff that has no immediate practical purpose for what I'm writing that day but which will come in handy perhaps later in the book or even in an entirely unrelated project.

I call this sort of thinking "gestating" with the allusion to pregnancy entirely intentional. With gestating thoughts I tend not to do anything with them until I know they're ready. I gestated the idea of *Old Man's War* for a couple of years until it became clear it was time to write it. I've got three or four big ideas gestating as we speak, and some are closer to popping out than others. There's no point rushing any of them. And what the means is that when they're ready to go, I've already lived with them for a long time. I think that cuts down the need to do a lot of rewriting to find the general shape of a story.

Now, having said all this, what will I do when my editors come back to me (as they inevitably will) and say: *This part needs to be rewritten?* Well, I'll rewrite it, of course. I know that just like I know how to do my job, my editor knows his job, and we both want the book to do well. As I've mentioned before, I'm not *precious* with my text. The words are words, not glistening jewels sparkling in the sunlight. Words are meant to do *work*. Things that work need to be told what to do and how to do it. Sometimes they're not doing it right. I did my job getting the work to the editor in as good a shape as possible, but I'm well aware that this only the first step in making it ready for an audience.

Nor do I think I'll *never* rewrite on my own. It's entirely possible at one point or another something I write is going to need a rewrite—I'd be stupid not to do it. I might have some ego wrapped up in not having done rewrites (it is kind of an unusual thing), but I have rather *more* ego wrapped up in not writing terrible stuff. My ego will get over rewriting something. But if I wrote a crappy book and it escaped into the world, I'd have to live with that for a real long time. If the choice is between rewrite and releasing crap, get me rewrite.

THE GRIPES
OF THE
UNPUBLISHED

(April 1, 2004)

H ere's an interesting comment to some writing advice I posted a couple of days ago, from someone
who chose to identify himself as "anonymous unpublished nobody":

> *I do appreciate the candor, however self-satisfy-*
> *ingly it was worded. I further appreciate the inspiration*
> *to never attempt to be published, if your view of the*
> *publishing industry rings true. If it is the frustrating*
> *job that you describe, it has lost its purpose in our*
> *society. I hate to sound like the hopeless romantic*
> *(okay, so I don't hate to…), but what good is the writing*
> *industry if all young dreamers with infinite and*
> *ultimately wasted potential have their pretty little*
> *illusions shattered by jaded workaholic laborers in*
> *what sounds like an occupational environment in a*
> *certain Fritz Lang film? We can include all the*
> *clever phrases and cultural name-dropping in our*
> *posts as we like, but what this seems to amount to is*
> *one self-important and bitter veteran's vitriolic rant*
> *against what he once was.*

The young and the unpublished may be silly and self-important and full of arrogant little illusions, but is it not better to fight for idealistic lost causes than to throw effort into a meaningless rat race under the guise of an artistic industry? Your publishing industry is just a mind-numbing entertainment industry. The publishing industry I see is a personal battlefield. The same questions you ask can be asked of you. You see the truth of what it takes to be "a writer." Why should I care? Someone is making more money than me as a writer because they publish photocopies of the same old novel. Why should I care? I may never get published. Why should I care? If an art becomes an industry, it has lost its purpose. And if a writer loses his illusions, however silly they are, then he has lost his ability to dream.

My response: Uh, *okay.*

I'll deal with the personal stuff first. As to the charge of self-importance: well, yeah. This is not news. As to the charge of bitterness: unlikely, since while there are people who could find the dark side of being able to do everything they ever wanted to do with their professional career, I'm personally not one of them. As to the charge of being angry at my younger self: also unlikely, as my younger self had basically the same approach to writing as my current self, which is, after all, a large part of why I am in the fortuitous writing position I am in at the moment. I would imagine if the me of today could talk to me when I was 21, the conversation would go something like this:

Me Now: Hey, just so you know, by the time you're thirty-five you'll have written six books, have been a nationally syndicated newspaper columnist, you'll review movies, music, and video games and get paid to spout off on whatever you feel like. And you'll be married to a super-hot babe and have a supercute kid, and they'll both be smarter than you are.

Me Then: Rock!

Me Now: Yes, exactly. Now give me your hair.

As to why this fellow should care what I think: beats me. As I've noted before, I readily admit to having my head up my ass. If someone readily admits to that, clearly the idea of *caveat emptor* is strongly implied.

So that's the easy part. Now let's talk about this thing about idealistic young writers being crushed by the unfeeling publishing world and needing their illusions, which, frankly, I'm not exactly sure I follow in the manner the writer intended. But let's give it the college try.

"Is it not better to fight for idealistic lost causes than to throw effort into a meaningless rat race under the guise of an artistic industry?"

Possibly, but even *better* to write what you want and then find an appropriate place to get it published. There are 1,600 magazines and 1,000 book publishers listed in my *2004 Writer's Market*. Provided you can actually string together sentences into paragraphs that don't demonstrably *suck*, there's a pretty good chance you can get published more or less on your own terms, particularly if you're not fussy about being paid a whole lot. Short of writing gay slash porn about the hot, moist love between Transformers and prehistoric trilobites ("Kekk the trilobite positioned himself on his back and opened his multiple legs welcomingly to Megatron, who began his erotic transformation. 'My God,' Kekk said, breathlessly. 'There really *is* more than meets the eye!'") most good writing can get sold.

"If an art becomes an industry, it has lost its purpose."
This makes a fabulous maxim to spout at your college coffee shop to that hot young black-clad Marxist you really want to sleep with, but what does it actually mean? One could easily argue that when art becomes an industry, it's an example of the democratization of aesthetics—bringing art to the people at affordable prices and thereby enriching the national discourse. In this scenario, if an art becomes an industry, it gains a purpose, does it not? I mean, come on—enriching the common man! That'll get you sex from your Marxist for sure.

My anonymous friend clearly has a bugaboo about "industry," but industry isn't inherently evil—industry merely implies systematized production and/or distribution of a particular good or service. Personally, I'm pretty happy about the idea of systematized production since that system gets what I write in front of more people than I could ever do myself; I'm lazy and I also don't have the time to hand-craft distribution deals with thousands of bookstores across the country.

The obvious rejoinder here is that industry also inevitably compresses choice—in a rush to get into the stores, publishers must anticipate and publish what sells as opposed to what's good. But aside from not being news at *all* (I imagine Gutenberg made Bibles because they sell well), I refer you again to the stat I quote above: 1,600 magazines and 1,000 book publishers. Your difficult but brilliant book may be an awful fit for a publisher who needs to sell 40,000 copies to break even but a perfect fit for an academic publisher who considers 1,000 copies sold to be a massive hit. Your trashy romance novel won't get past the gate at one publisher but might be madly embraced at another.

"And if a writer loses his illusions, however silly they are, then he has lost his ability to dream."

Oh, please. Get a *grip*. I can't even begin to count all the ways this line doesn't make the slightest bit of sense.

But here's one: Illusions, by definition, are false—and therefore not at all useful for a writer to have. Writers with illusions about their talent, or about the state of publishing, or about life in general are bound to be continually disappointed, because the real world doesn't care about your illusions. On the other hand, if you know what you're good at, know how things get published and have a good grip on your general situation, you're in an excellent position to make your writing dreams come true, inasmuch as they involve actually being professionally published.

I'll tell you one true thing, which is that I spend a lot of my time recently thinking about what I'm going to write next—the next batch of book ideas I'm going to send to my agents to make the rounds, as well as some book ideas that I'm fairly sure my agents won't see as salable but which I suspect I'll probably fiddle with anyway because I *want* to, and who cares if they can sell them or not (there's always the Web site). Point is, I don't have much in the way of illusions regarding the business of writing. Yet strangely enough, that doesn't stop me from having quite a few dreams.

I think the fundamental problem that this anonymous dude might have is simply that he seems to think writing is too dear for the predations of the real world. Well, whatever. I really don't know what to tell people who sort of airily go off about how writing is this great, honest pure thing that has been subjugated to the banal ravishments of the soulless machine known as "publishing," but I suppose that's because my relationship with the muse has always been, shall we say, a *pragmatic* one. People often ask me when it was I knew I wanted to be a writer, and I usually tell them it was when I was in my first year of high school, when I realized that for me writing was really easy and most other things (math, languages, getting dates) were kind of *hard*. And so I—and I remember this very clearly—made the conscious decision that what I was going to do was focus on being a writer because writing well meant *I could avoid real work*.

So I can say that from the very beginning my desire to write was intensely practical: being a good writer meant I might make a living being a writer, which meant I could avoid doing the things I didn't want to do (i.e., damn near everything else). That's what I did. So far, it's worked pretty well. I'm hardly bitter about where it's taken me. Most of the time, I'm having *fun*.

REAL WORLD
BOOK DEAL
DESCRIPTIONS

(September 8, 2004)

Now, I've recently come back from the Noreascon science fiction convention, and if you've ever read one of my convention recaps, you may have come away thinking that most of what writers do at conventions is drinking and carousing and then possibly drinking some more. And you'd be right. However, I don't want you to think that nothing of value was accomplished there—or indeed that nothing of value can be accomplished even while drinking.

As proof of this, it gives me great pride to introduce to the world the **Real World Book Deal Descriptions**, as formulated at Noreascon 4 at the Sheraton Hotel Lobby Bar by a group of only somewhat inebriated writers including Scott Westerfeld, Justine Larbalestier, Kelly Link, James Patrick Kelly, Lauren McLaughlin, Eliani Torres, Shara Zoll and your humble narrator. A couple others were there as well, but the point is, this is group wisdom, based on decades of collective writing experience.

Now, some background. One of the most widely-read e-mail lists in publishing is Publisher's Lunch, in which various book deals are announced with certain euphemisms to describe what sort of money was involved. For example, book deals that get the writer up to $100,000 are known as "a nice deal." $100K to $250 is "a good deal," and so on up past the $1 million point, at which you have "a major deal." And well, yes, if you're up at that point, it certainly *is* a major deal, you bastard.

Thing is, for most writers (and I include myself here), about 80% of those levels never get used: The vast majority of book publishing deals are "nice." However, using one adjective to describe both the $1,000 book deal someone gets from a teeny university press and the $90,000 book deal from a major New York publisher is obviously ridiculous. A $1K book deal and a $90K book deal are quite clearly not equivalent; one is, oh, *90 times better* than the other. If only for sheer honesty's sake, there needs to be book deal rankings that accurately reflect what deals really get done and the financial quality of those deals for the writer.

So, after another round of beers, this is what we came up with.

$0 to $3,000: A Shitty Deal. Because that's what it is, my friends. Possibly the only thing worse than a shitty deal is no deal at all. *Possibly*.

$3,000 to $5,000: A Contemptible Deal. The deal you get when your publisher has well and truly got your number, and it is low.

$5,000 to $10,000: A *"Meh"* Deal. It's not *great*, you know. But you can pay some bills. Get a few of these, and a tolerant spouse with a regular income, and you can tell your day job to piss off. This year, anyway.

$10,000 to $20,000: A Not Bad Deal. Note that "not bad" here should be said with a slight appreciative rise of the eyebrows and a small approving nod—this is the level at which the money begins to look not embarrassing both to writers and non-writers. A couple of these, and you'll definitely be punting the day job (I did, anyway).

$20,000 to $100,000: A "Shut Up!" Deal. This needs to be said in the same enviously admiring vocal tone as a teenage girl might use to her girlfriend who is showing off the delicious new pumps she got at Robinsons-May for 30% off, or the vocal tone (same idea, lower register) Jim Kelly used when one of our number admitted to having at least a couple of deals in this range. With this kind of money, you don't even *need* a supportive spouse to avoid the Enforced Top Ramen Diet (although, you know. Having one doesn't *hurt*). But it's not so much that the other writers actively begin to *hate* you.

$100,000 and above: "I'm Getting the Next Round." Because if you're at this level, you can buy and sell all the other writers at the table. Get 'em a friggin' beer, for God's sake (ironically, this is the only level not thought up at the bar, but in the cold hard light of the next morning, by Shara Zoll).

Think how much more interesting and useful the Publisher's Lunch would be if these rankings were used:
"Joe Wannabe's THE FIRST NOVEL IS THE MOST ANNOYING, a coming-of-age story about a not particularly interesting 20-something graduate student who is eventually dumped by his girlfriend for being a mopey, emo-listening sack of crap, to Random Small Press, in a shitty deal."

"Susan Midlist's THE MARY SUE CRITICAL MASS, the story of a world thrown into chaos when large numbers of bookish women spontaneously appear at critical events of historical importance and passive-aggressively demand to play a role, to Not Insignificant Genre Press, in a *meh* deal."

"Neil Popular's A DARK UNIVERSE FULL OF CASH, a tale of a man who wakes up one morning with fame and fortune but then must tolerate being accosted at random intervals by strangers who want to be his best friends and/or to have him blurb their own work, to Big Respected Publisher. He'll get the next round."

See, that's *much* better.

For the record, Nightshade Books is an excellent small press, and its publisher Jeremy Lassen is a fine fellow. But he can be confrontational in his opinions (just ask him!), and here I'm confrontational back. —JS

WHY A SHITTY DEAL IS A SHITTY DEAL

(September 14, 2004)

A small press publisher named Jeremy Lassen, who is clearly not getting enough hugs, took exception to the Real World Book Deals definition of a $3,000 book advance as "shitty," and responded with a comment which I'll elevate here for you to admire as much for the spirited use of profanity as the content itself. In it, Lassen also tries to suggest that authors really don't want a $20K advance, or above. Follow the logic, such as it is:

$3,000 advance = the expectation of selling at least 1,200 copies of a $27 hardcover at 10% royalty.

That's 2,400 copies of a trade paperback at $13.50.

For a small publisher with a first time author's fiction book, those are pretty respectable numbers. Shitty deal my ass. Particularly if you still have a piece of paperback, foreign language, or British rights.

A $20,000 advance = "not bad?" Fuck that. A $20,000 advance could mean the end of your fucking career. If you don't sell 7,500 copies of your book in hardcover, or 15,000 of your book in trade paperback, you didn't earn out. If you don't earn out, chances are your publisher just lost money on your ass, and your editor is getting heat from above. Chances are that editor is telling everybody in town what a bad investment you were...

Now if that had been a $5,000 advance, and you sold half that—3,200 copies, your book would have earned out and made a bit of money, and would have been a good investment, and would probably get you another contract.

If you actually sold 7,500 copies after a $5,000 advance, you would have been a long shot that paid off big. Your editor would look like a genius, and you might get a 2 book deal, and...AND YOU WOULD HAVE STILL ENDED UP EARNING $2OK on the first book, after royalties were paid.

Let's be realistic people. If your book sells, you get paid. If your book doesn't sell, and you still got a big fat advance up front, chances are you won't ever get a contract with that publisher again. If you think you can sell more copies than your publisher thinks they can, don't sell it to them, or self publish it, if there's so much demand.

Fucking unrealistic expectations are part of the problem in this industry. Arbitrary lists like this perpetuate this shit. It's more important to understand the economics of your trade (advances, royalties, trade discounts, distributor discounts, returns, Pay-for-placement in chains, etc etc), rather then memorizing some arbitrary range of "advances" and whether it was a good deal or not.

The problem is most writers don't know shit about the business they are in, and assfucks like Publishers Lunch don't seem to be interested in helping them learn anything about it.

Aside from the clear contempt Lassen has for writers, whom he apparently assumes are too stupid/ignorant to follow basic publishing economics, Lassen misses two critical points about the Real World Publishing Deal list:

1. It's primarily supposed to be funny and satirical (although as with most funny and/or satirical things, there's a small bit of truth to it). For the purposes of my little essay here, however, let's go ahead and treat it seriously.

2. It's a list from the perspective of the writer, not the perspective of the publisher—as befits its creation by a *bunch of writers* hanging around at a bar. And here's a fact, for writers and publishers both: When the cost of your bar tab from a night of carousing with other writers is an integral percentage of your book advance, that's a pretty shitty advance, no matter how you slice it.

Likewise, if Lassen doesn't think $3,000 is a shitty deal for writing a book, he's welcome to try to live off it. I doubt he'll get a good Internet connection from an underpass.

To be clear, the "shitty" aspect of tiny advances as described in or little list relates to one thing: the raw amount of money involved. The small press publisher who offers you $3,000 or less for your book may sincerely be offering the most amount of money he or she can offer; likewise, a writer may be eminently pleased to take that dinky sum for a number of reasons. Money is not the only thing involved in a book deal.

Be that as it may, here and *now*, $3K is a shitty amount of money. It's shitty in exchange for the amount of labor involved in writing a book, and it's shitty in the real world of paying rent, buying groceries and keeping the lights on. $3K is a nickel a word (or less, if you write more than 60,000 words). If you live in New York City or San Francisco and don't have rent control, $3K is a writer's monthly "nut"—i.e., your cost of living (note to writers: Get the hell out of NYC and SF).

Lassen's exhortations of paltry book economics aside, no author *wants* to make $3,000 or less from their work. It's "I won't bring up what I was paid to the parents who wanted me to be an accountant" money. It's "I'll never be able to give up my day job" money. It's "I'm glad I've got a tolerant partner" money. An author may take $3K (or less) for an advance, and may even be happy with the deal—but dollars to donuts they're not actually happy with the raw money. And why should they be? To repeat: it's a shitty amount of money.

(Let's not also fall for Lassen's intimation that authors will make more money on the backend through royalties; most books don't earn out, even the ones with the small advances. And unless the book in question is a wild success, the royalty money will be hella slow in coming—it can be years before authors see a royalty statement. One of the best pieces of advice I can give to an author is to think of your advance as *all the money you will ever get for your book*. It keeps you from the credit card mentality of "I'll do 'X' when 'Y' money comes in." And it makes the royalty money you do get even more pleasant.)

Lassen's frantic handwaving about how a $20K advance could torpedo your career, incidentally, is a load of crap. He's doing what he accuses us writers of doing, which is plucking a more or less arbitrary number out of the air and declaring it good or bad. As it happens, I got a $20,000 advance for my very first book (*The Rough Guide to Money Online*). I've gotten contracts for six books since then—some whose advances are more, some that are less. In my case, $20,000 was a perfectly reasonable amount for an advance. For some people $20K will be too much; for others, not near enough.

And in fact, the story of *Money Online* is a fine example of how both publishers and authors view advances. At the time I was contracted to write *Money Online*, Rough Guide's Internet guide had sold hugely—more than a million copies—and from what I was told, the company was expecting pretty large sales of *Money Online* as well. Because of that, the $20K advance the company extended was viewed as a safe—nay, cheap!—bet. But as it happened, the book came out in November of 2000, i.e., just in time for the popping of the Internet bubble. The book's sales were in the thousands, not the hundreds of thousands, and I didn't earn out my advance. It was bad timing.

Yet my second book sale was to Rough Guides as well—*The Rough Guide to the Universe*. Why did RG go with me again, even though my first book was a clear financial disappointment? Well, for a number of reasons, I imagine. First and not insignificantly, the number of books an author needs to sell to earn out an advance and the number of books a publisher needs to sell to turn a profit (or at least avoid a loss) are *not* the same number, which is a point of fact Lassen doesn't bother to point out (but then, why would he). It's my understanding that RG didn't actually lose any money on the book. So that's good. Second, despite the first book's failure to thrive in the marketplace, the folks at RG liked the book's content and liked me as a writer; they were not shy about working with me again. Third, the *Universe* book filled a hole in their offerings. So there it was.

As it happens, the advance RG offered for *Universe* was less than for *Money Online*. I didn't squawk—the step down was not huge, and in light of the *Money Online* sales, not at all unreasonable. Also, I really wanted to write a book on astronomy. Everyone was happy with the deal. *Universe* sold well and was reviewed well; now I'm writing another book for Rough Guides, and the money involved has gone up.

Point here, to borrow from William Goldman: *Nobody knows anything*. Great books can fail, bad books can thrive; your advance money may seem like a bargain to your publisher today but arterial flow tomorrow, or vice versa; the small press publisher who offers you $1,500 for your book and then takes a bath on it may never work with you again; the large publisher who offers up $150,000 for another book may chuckle quietly into his bourbon about how he got the book for silly cheap. The idea that a writer should be content with a paltry advance, however, is a load of crap. The advance a writer should be content with is the one that is the happy medium between what the writer thinks he or she is worth and what the publisher think it can sell. Any *other* advance is someone screwing someone else.

This much is true: The economics of publishing from the point of view of the writer and the point of view of the publisher are related but *they are not the same*. The publisher looks at the economics of publishing from the point of view of needing to create and market product; the writer looks from the point of view of eating. To some extent the publisher's costs are fungible—how many books to print, where to advertise, whether to fund a book tour and so on. The writer's costs, on the other hand, are fungible across a much smaller range (a gallon of milk costs about the same wherever you go). The publisher's view of economics is institutional; the writer's, personal.

Lassen suggests, in a rather obnoxious fashion, that writers need a dose of reality when it comes to publishing economics. The subtext message in his bloviation is clear: the only *legitimate* point of view for the economics of publishing is that of the publisher. This is of course *entirely* wrong. We writers are not ignorant of the economics of publishing; we are, if anything, only too *well* acquainted with them. Our point of view matters and is indeed singularly relevant, since without writers, publishing has a real supply problem.

This is why a gaggle of writers, only slightly in their cups, unanimously declared certain deals "Shitty," "Contemptible." "Meh," and so on. From our point of view, that's a fair referent for the money involved and what it can do for us. I can buy shit for $1,000, so a $1,000 deal is pretty shitty. I can pay my mortgage for a year on $20,000. That's not bad. And the day I get a deal worth $100,000 or more, I'm definitely buying the next round. Really, I don't know how much clearer this can be.

It's probably that Lassen doesn't like the amount of money he can (or is willing to) offer as an advance referred to as "shitty." Well, I can sympathize, but only up to a point. If the economics of publishing are such that shitty or contemptible pay is what writers can hope to expect, then there's no point pretending otherwise. At the very least, everyone who *wants* to be a writer will know what they're getting themselves into.

NOVELIST MONEY

(December 24, 2004)

Justine Larbalestier, whose perfectly fabulous YA novel is coming out in a few months, asked some author friends of hers what sort of advance they got for their first novels, because she's curious and because enough people Googled her site to find out that she felt she might as well have the information posted up there. The results of her informal polling, added to a rather more extensive list of what romance publishers provide for advances, gives one the general indication that very few people who are not already famous (or related to someone famous) get a whole lot of advance money for their first works, particularly in genre markets. But then, if you hang out here, you should have known about that already.

However, for me, this was the paragraph I found most interesting:

> *Of the 18 people I asked, only seven are full-time writers (no, Samuel R. Delany is not one of them, he earns his dosh as a university professor) and of those only two of them are doing fine (New York Times' bestseller, Shut-up! or I'm-getting-the-next-round advances fine—definitely no longer worrying about where the next cheque is coming from). The rest are in their words "scraping by" or "barely comfortable" and depend overly much on their credit cards, except for Scalzi who is smart enough to also make money writing non-fiction.*

Yup. Non-fiction and also corporate and newspaper/ magazine work; if I had to rely only on the money I get for books under my own name, I'd be doing a lot *less* fine, both in terms of raw income and in terms of spreading out the income I did get throughout the year. Bills come on a regular cycle, even if book money doesn't. Although book-writing income has become a greater percentage of my writing income, at the end of the day it's still the minority.

And the income from *fiction* writing—which at this point is purely advance money—is a small enough amount that, to be quite blunt about it, I pretty much forgot I was owed an advance on *The Android's Dream* until my wife Krissy (who manages the money around here, and thank God) reminded me and told me to pester Tor about it. As a functional part of my income (i.e., the part that pays bills, mortgages and other such things), my fiction advances are not a consideration, and at the level that I'm paid for fiction at the moment, if it *did* become part of my functional income, I imagine I'd be pretty concerned. I'd need to both lower my expenses and raise my income.

Would I like to get larger advances writing fiction? Well, sure, and I am; I'm getting more for *The Ghost Brigades*, for example (for *Android's Dream* I made the same amount as for OMW). But unless I become a major-selling author, and reliably so, it would be unrealistic to assume I will get eye-popping advances, and in any event it will take a few years to see where I stand in terms of moving books off the shelves. In other words, even if I do get to continue to publish fiction (and I hope I do), realistically I expect fiction advances to be one of the smaller segments of my income pie for some time to come.

And if it stays a small portion of my income, well, I'm fine with that. One doesn't get to the income level I'm at without being money conscious (and reasonably not-stupid about money) but neither am I wholly money-motivated, particularly when it comes to writing fiction; the fact I put *Old Man's War* on my Web site to begin with, rather than shop it to publishers, bolsters this point. I want to make money with my fiction, yes. But what I really want to do with my fiction is write some really good stories. If I make a lot of money, swell. If no one buys them and I post them here and get not a single red cent, that's fine, too. It's nice to be in a financial position where I can do either and not have to count my change walking away.

(Note to publishers: Please do not assume this means I'll be happy being low-balled. My agent is likely to correct such misapprehensions.)

THE MONEY INVOLVED

(February 9, 2005)

Someone asked in one of the comment threads: If the first printing of *Old Man's War* sells out, will I have earned out my advance? So I crunched the numbers and the answer is: Yeah, it looks like it—the first print run was about 3,800 copies, and my math shows my break-even point at 2,700 or 3,400 copies, depending on what royalty rate you use (I could pin down the royalty rate by looking at the contract, but then I'd have to dig it out, and that would take too much effort) Even a worst case scenario (which has me signing a contract that offers a 6% royalty, because I was high on cough syrup or some such) would have me earning out after about 4,500 copies sold, and it seems reasonably likely at this point OMW will hit that target while still in hardback.

This is a good thing, obviously. One, it means paperback royalties go into my pocket, and that's likely where the majority of money is to be made; two, if I'm breaking even on the hardback that means Tor is almost certainly making money. And as a general rule, you want to make money for your publishers. It encourages them to publish you again, and I'm all for being published again.

Now, the fact that I will have earned out with such a relatively small number of books sold should indicate something to the more observant among you: either I have a truly extravagant royalty rate, or my advance was pretty small. Well, I don't have an extravagant royalty rate, I in fact have a rather pedestrian one, so that points to a small advance. And indeed, it's well within the "*meh*" range by "real world advances" formulation. However, I should note I'm just fine with this, and I'll tell you why.

Meet author Sam Lipsyte. Mr. Lipsyte is the star of an article I've just recently read, in which we learn about the Herculean struggle he had to get his second novel published here in the United States (he ended up having to get it published in the UK, to rave reviews, before someone would bite over here in the states). Why was it so difficult to sell his second novel? Well, it could be because, by all indications, Mr. Lipsyte is a writer whose prose one either loves or hates, which is a strike against him at least 50% of the time, and also his quirky style makes him difficult to quantify, which will drive the marketing people right up a wall. But more likely it was because the publisher of his first novel gave Lipsyte a $60,000 advance for his first novel, and the first novel stiffed. Big time.

Perspective: To earn out a $60,000 advance, Lipsyte would have had to sell 25,104 copies of his book at 10% royalty, or 31,413 copies at 8%. Any amount under that, he'd have to make up in the paperback sales, where the price (and thus the royalty) is lower. More perspective: for mainstream fiction, 25,000 copies is considered bestseller status (if what I read in the *New York Times* is correct).

While it is entirely possible for a first-time novelist to become a bestseller, the actual odds are pretty grim. It's even *less* likely if reviewers keep comparing you to somewhat inaccessible writers (Thomas Pynchon, for example) and warn readers that "the characters here don't so much converse as exchange obtuse epigrammatic non sequiturs and indulge in linguistic quips." Basically, Lipsyte probably got hosed because his publishers spent too much money for a book that was deeply unlikely to earn out its advance. And it didn't—it sold 5,000 copies.

And so his next book, *Home Land*, sold in the US—when it sold—for a quarter of what he got for the first one: $15,000. As it happens, the book came out the very same day as mine did, and by all indications is selling in numbers not dissimilar to my own; the article notes it's sold 2,000 copies to date, which is in the same ball park as mine. Here's the thing: If I sell 5,000 copies, I'm a success, at least as far as the rubric of earning out your advance is concerned. Lipsyte, on the other hand, is still underwater at 5,000 copies; he's underwater until he gets to 11,500 copies (presuming 10% royalty). If he doesn't get there, he's a two-time commercial loser, which would likely make it that much harder to get to book number three.

Bear in mind this has *nothing* to do with Lipsyte's talent as a writer. He may indeed be wonderful to read, and it's quite likely he *should* be read by a wider audience. What I'm saying is that if he and I—both writers in our mid-thirties, both in relatively the same place in our writing careers—both were to sell, say, 10,000 copies of our latest book, I'd be seen as a happy success by my publisher, and he'd be seen (whatever his talent) as a mild disappointment, and the only real difference between us—commercially speaking, anyway—is a few thousand dollars in advance money.

Which does bring up the question—why *did* this guy get a $60,000 advance for his first novel, and I only a rather small fraction of that sum? Is he many multiples better than I as a writer? Alternately, is his fiction a multiple more salable than mine? As toward the latter, evidently *not*, and for the former, it's certainly possible, but probably irrelevant. I suspect a more likely answer is simply that Lipsyte writes literary fiction whereas I write genre fiction, and anecdotally speaking it appears that publishers are willing to pay more for literary fiction than for genre fiction.

One does of course wonder, if this *is* true, why that might be—I would love to have someone slap down the sales figures for genre writers and for lit fic writers and show me whether the average and median sales for each justify either the high advances for literary fiction, or the low advances for genre fiction. I rather strongly suspect that what we'd find is that literary fiction is overvalued as to its commercial prospects relative to genre fiction, for no better reason than snobbery toward little green men (I can possibly accept an argument that literary fiction is, on average, more *literary* than genre fiction, but being "literary" is just one portion of being "readable," and as we all know there's a lot of literary fiction that's well nigh unreadable. Also, I suspect that China Mieville and Neil Gaiman, to name just two, are as resolutely "lit'ry" as anyone, *and* yet still readable, so there's nothing to suggest genre work can't be eminently literary as well).

In any event, I'm not entirely sure I want to take a position that non-genre authors ought to be dragged down to genre authors' rather meager pay scales; I'm pretty sure that won't make me a lot of friends. And God knows I'm not criticizing Lipsyte for taking the $60k when it was offered to him, because, you know, I'd not be likely to turn it down, either. I do think, however, that publishers aren't doing first-time non-genre authors any favors by offering them advances they're not likely to recoup and then branding the poor bastards as uncommercial when they don't. That really is blaming the victim. Either literary fiction editors are absolutely clueless about money, or they simply don't care and are happy to spend stupidly. Either way, I would probably fire these editors and replace them with editors trained in genre fiction; I suspect that after the shock had worn off in the lit fic community, the corporate parents of book publishers would find a modest uptick in their bottom lines.

My advance for *Old Man's War* was small, but as it turns out it's pretty much what it should have been for me, both for the short-term happy accomplishment of earning out my advance and for the longer-term goal of beginning to establish myself as a commercially viable author. Do I want to get a bigger advance next time out? You bet—and, as it happens, for *The Ghost Brigades*, I got one. That's the way it's supposed to work, and so far it's working for me.

CREATIVE COMMONS AND FANFIC

(April 11, 2005)

Welcome everyone to the Whatever's annual Reader Request Week, in which readers suggest a topic, and then I blather on about it. To start things off, let's combine two requests that go well together. Chris asks:

> *Intellectual property—Where do you feel an equitable compromise lies in the fair-use/right-of-artists-to-profit-from-their-work debate? Any thoughts on the Creative Commons license, specifically as pertains to your future work? (Cory Doctorow released a couple of his novels online and in dead-tree form simultaneously, while Orson Scott Card did okay for himself with the Shadow series by releasing the first few chapters of each a few months ahead of the street date. Any plans to do something similar?)*

And to this I'll add a related question from **Night Dog**:

> *I'd like to know what you think of fanfiction. Do you think it's a legitimate exercise of imagination, or a trampling on copyright?*

To my mind (and, as it happens, as more or less stated in

the Constitution of the United States) copyright exists for two purposes: first, to make sure the creator benefits from having a thought or two; second, to make sure that (eventually) the public sphere is enriched by the work of that creator. Problems arise, of course, at the extremes—when people download all the music in Western civilization off of KaZaa, for example, and get indignant at the idea they're doing something *wrong*, or when Disney pays off the US Congress yet again to make sure Mickey Mouse never gets his Emancipation Proclamation, and as a result copyright terms are extended far beyond their original intent and (more importantly) to the detriment of the commons.

In my perfect copyright world, I'd have a simple scheme for copyrights: For copyrights held by individuals, copyrights would last for 50 years or the life of the individual plus 25 years (to benefit widowed spouses and heirs), whichever is longer. For work owned by corporations, 75 years and out. But I would *also* add a provision that after the initial copyright, the copyright holder could renew the copyright annually for the sum of 2 to the x power, where "x" is equal to the current year past the original copyright expiration, with the monies raised going (initially, at least) to US deficit reduction.

So, for example, if the copyright on "Steamboat Willie" were to expire today, Disney could pay $2 for a one year extension of the copyright. In 2015, it would have to pay $1,024. In 2025, $1,048,576. And in 2035, $1,073,741,824. By which time, of course, Disney would have finally let "Steamboat Willie" steam on to public domain. Now, given the sheer number of copyrights that Disney alone would have to protect on an annual basis, you can see how **a)** the corporation would have to pick and choose which things to maintain under copyright longer than their original term, thereby freeing other material sooner, and **b)** how quickly a scheme like this would pay down the deficit—without raising taxes!—thus benefiting the public sphere even without the public domain use of the intellectual property. Naturally, I expect you to contact your Congressperson right this very second and demand that he / she offer up the Scalzi Copyright Enhancement Act of 2005 as soon as humanly possible. You know, for the kids.

Now, having thus addressed the philosophical issue of what the lengths of copyrights should be and how to find the balance between the rights of the copyright holder and the public, let's address the issue of ownership under copyright. Naturally, being a copyright owner myself, I wish to have and retain the full protections of that copyright: If someone's taking my stuff without my permission and making a buck from it, I want to be able to nail his ass; likewise, if someone is distributing my work for free in a manner in which I do not approve, I want to be able to legally stop her from doing so as well, especially if it is having a negative impact on my financial bottom line. It is *my* work, damn it. I should have the right to control it, and legally I do.

At the same time, I don't think there's any value in being an intellectual property dickhead, either. What non-creative bean-counters don't get that many creative people do is that many of the things that will lose you money in the short term, intellectual property-wise, will gain you money in the long term, because it creates a *fan*—someone who is actively looking for your next creative work, and many of whom, because they feel that personal connection with you, will happily pay for that next work.

Certainly I've benefited from it, primarily from the Whatever, my own person writing site. I've been giving away work there for six years, including a full-length novel, and partially as a result of that, my first published novel is now in its fourth printing. Check out the comments in the *Agent to the Stars* guestbook and some of the most common things you'll see there are variations of "thanks for letting me check this out for free—I'll be looking for your published stuff now." (Let's also not forget that both *Agent* and *Old Man's War* found their way to actual publication because they were available to be read online—no if ands or buts about it.) I'm a big believer in keeping active control of the work I produce, but part of that control is the freedom to *share* that work with whomever I choose.

It's paid off for me, and it's paid off for others, too. All of Cory Doctorow's published novels are available online for free and he'd certainly maintain it's been a boon to the sales of his books. Orson Scott Card did indeed post not just chapters but full novels online at one point (I know because I downloaded *Children of the Mind* off his AOL forum) until apparently persuaded otherwise by his publisher (who is, interestingly, the same publisher who let Cory post his works online—but OSC's experience was several years back in the timestream, and times have emphatically changed). Baen Books famously has its Free Library with dozens of books, and it claims that having these out there does indeed drive sales. Being open with your work *works*.

(BUT—is there a bend in the curve after which it *doesn't?* Aside from corporate hysteria, this is an interesting question. For example, my having a full novel online is only a net positive because, aside from y'all, I'm a complete unknown; even in its fourth printing, there are still fewer than 10,000 copies of OMW out there. Cory is somewhat significantly better known than I, as his site Boing Boing has rather higher readership, he's a luminary in the intellectual property arena and he's been publishing longer than I—and yet he is also a mid-listy sort of writer at this point (saleswise). Again, the publicity is a net positive.

But what about someone like Orson Scott Card, who sells hundreds of thousands of books annually, and whose work is never *not* on the science fiction shelves at your local bookstore? Does the same dynamic that Cory and I use to our advantage work in the same way for someone at his sales level? Or does it simply cannibalize his sales? Bearing in mind I have *no* idea of Tor's point of view on this, I could see a publisher who easily tolerates online experiments from new writers and mid-listers getting twitchy if one of their main draws started flirting with giving stuff away for free online.

The same goes for music: indie musicians who haven't a chance getting on the radio have nothing to lose and everything to gain by letting people download songs for free. A major label artist who has to recoup a million dollars in studio fees—or the label that advanced those fees and owns the masters—may feel differently. Everyone's looking for the bend in the curve, and naturally the more money you have in the till, the more significant it is to you.)

As for Creative Commons, it's unlikely that I'll do any significant work and release it under CC. It's not that I'm unsympathetic to the aims of CC; intellectually speaking I like the concept of giving people a series of blanket permissions to rework your work, and if that's what you want to do, go for it. Nor is it that I don't want people to fiddle with what I write or create; generally speaking, I'd be flattered. What it comes down to for me is that I want to know what people are doing with my stuff ahead of time. If someone wants to do a "remix" of *Agent to the Stars*, say, it would not be onerous for them to send me an e-mail first and ask permission. I am not so unapproachable that such communication is impossible.

But to reverse an earlier formulation: I often choose to be free with the work I create, but that choice is mine to make. I prefer to make such choices actively rather than passively.

All of this dovetails interestingly into the concept of "fanfic"—which for those of you who are not SF geeks, means creative writing done borrowing already-created characters and situations from popular media. *Star Trek* is, to mix progenitor metaphors, the granddaddy motherlode of fanfic, but suffice to say wheresoever two or more fans gather to share an obsessive love of TV, movies, music, literature or video games, so there also shall be fanfic. Fanfic is of course a massive violation of copyright, since all of a sudden Spock and Kirk are doing things Viacom never intended them to do (or Darth Vader and Yoda, or Buffy and Willow, or Harry Potter and Hermione, or Mario and Luigi or whatever), and naturally this gets the corporate IP lawyers all het up.

Honestly, though, if I were the creator of a science fiction or fantasy media property (as opposed to a mere book author) and I didn't find evidence of fanfic online, I would be *very* worried. People don't write fanfic if they aren't already so enthralled by your universe that they can't handle the fact you're not producing it any faster, and are thus compelled to make some of their own—the methadone, if you will, to your pure, sweet media property heroin. A fanfic writer will buy all your media-related product, will go to your conventions, will get the DVDs and will generally slog through sub-standard and lazy stretches of your work far longer than the average mortal because they are so damn invested. And if they're writing slash (fanfic with sex!), chances are excellent that you're sucking in all of their take home pay that doesn't go to rent, food and cat products. It is the Buffy slash writers who paid for

Joss Whedon's boat (or whatever other particularly silly display of wealth that he's purchased for himself).

So as a creator, if I ever see the appearance of fanfic based on something I wrote, I'm going to be tickled seven different shades of pink, and then I'm going to make a down payment on a Mercedes. Because man, *now* I can afford it. So, please, off with the lot of you. Go write some OMW fanfic! Rather more seriously, as a creator I probably wouldn't go out of my way to squash fanfic, because it's essentially harmless and not a real economic danger. If I became aware that someone was *selling* their fanfic, I might have my lawyers slip them a note reminding them that he/she didn't have the right to do that, and to stop. Unless it was *really* good, in which case I'd probably buy it and market it. Hey, video game makers hire programmers who started out making "mods" of their favorite games. So why not.

As a writer, I also have no opposition to fanfic. I understand that many writers who write fanfic have no real ambition to be writers aside from the specific fanfic they write—it's a slightly more intellectual version of playing with dolls, and therefore its own end, and it doesn't really matter what the quality is. For the fanfic writers who do actually want to *be* writers, I think there are advantages and disadvantages.

The advantages are that you're writing in an established universe with established characters whose qualities and failings are well known to you; all you have to do is plug them into a situation and play the changes. It's easier than coming up with something whole cloth—and therefore arguably an easy way to play with the mechanics of writing since the story comes partially built. It's writing with training wheels.

The disadvantage is the same: You're working in someone else's universe, and there's only so far you can go with that.

Eventually you're going to have to leave the safe sandbox of the Federation or the New Republic or Buffy. Since I don't write fan fiction, I don't know how difficult that is. There's also the issue that since no one will buy fanfic except under extremely rare circumstances (for obvious copyright reasons), writers playing in the fanfic world deprive themselves of a necessary step in any writers' evolution: Working with editors.

If people are writing fanfic simply for fun, I see very little harm in it, although this is *not* the response you'll get from an IP lawyer. If people are writing fanfic to become better writers, they should be writing other stuff, since it's the other stuff that will get them published. And ironically enough, once they're published on their own, there's a non-trivial chance they'll be approached to do a media tie-in novel! It's the circle of fanfic, and it moves us all.

THE STUPIDITY OF WORRYING ABOUT PIRACY

(May 13, 2005)

The Science Fiction and Fantasy Writers of America, to which I belong, recently e-mailed its members a poll about Amazon's "look within the book" feature, about how they felt about it and whether they'd want to let Amazon browsers check out their books online—and how much of the book they'd want to let people read. It's a perfectly legitimate question, and I think that it should be up to the writers and publishers to make that decision. But whomever it is that wrote the poll (I assume Andrew Burt, as it's hosted on his site) is apparently so paranoid about piracy that they've felt it was perfectly fine to add editorial comment in the poll itself warning about the dangers of Amazon-borne piracy.

For example, one question asking how much of a work one would want to have accessible to Amazon browsers is phrased this way: "What percent would you want blocked of your work to prevent piracy?" I'm not a professional pollster, but I know a push poll question when I see it, and I don't like it any more when it comes from SFWA than when it comes from a political party.

My response to the poll, incidentally, was that I wanted *all* of the book available for Amazon shoppers to browse. I want this for many reasons, not the least of which is simply parity of shopping experience to bookstores, where one can go up to the bookshelves, crack open a book, and read as much of it as one wants to see if one is interested in making a purchase. As it happens, I don't buy very many books online because I *can't* open the book and see the text, and with new writers especially, I'm not going to buy without checking out the book first.

Now, flip this over: *I'm* a new writer and I know for a fact that a rather substantial percentage of my sales have been online sales, thanks to the fact that so many purchases of *Old Man's War* have been driven by bloggers, and because for various reasons the book has been damned hard to find in actual bookstores (there's never been a single copy in *my* local bookstore, for example). Why would I shoot my sales in the foot by not letting readers browse my book, just as much as they'd like to browse, just like they would be able to do in a brick and mortar store?

The quick and obvious answer to this—if one is paranoid about piracy—is that in a brick and mortar store, someone can't take a screen capture of your book, run it through software and make a readable text file of your book that they then post on KaZaa, *arrrrrr*, for all their scurvy friends to read for free. And the answer to this is: Well, jeez, people. As if that very same would-be pirate couldn't check out my book from the *library* and do the same damn thing with a scanner. I'm not terribly convinced that doing a screen capture of *every single page* of my book on Amazon is any *less* work than scanning in every single page of a print copy.

Banning people from reading my book on Amazon is unlikely to deter someone who is truly motivated to pirate my book, and to scan every single friggin' page—however one does it—you have to be pretty goddamn motivated. You'd also have to pretty motivated to read my entire book through Amazon's less-than-entirely-user-friendly text preview tool. Most people just aren't going to do that, and the ones that are, I'm not going to sell to anyway. I'm not going to punish the people who are likely to buy my book on the off chance that I might temporarily inconvenience someone who *won't*. That's just stupid. So: I'll let Amazon show off the entire book. I don't see how it can hurt me, and I see lots of ways it can *help* me.

Does this mean I run the risk of being pirated? Well, clearly it does. But let take a nice cold shower and look at this logically, shall we?

Let's ask: Who are pirates? They are people who *won't* pay for things (i.e., dickheads), or they're people who *can't* pay for things (i.e., cash-strapped college students and others). The dickheads have ever been with us; they wouldn't pay even if they had the money. I don't worry about them, I just hope they fall down an abandoned well, break their legs and die of gangrene after several excruciatingly painful days of misery and dehydration, and then I hope the rats chew the marrow from their bones and shit back down the hollows. And that's that for them.

As for the people who *can't* pay for things, well, look. I grew up poor and made music tapes off the radio; my entire music collection from ages 11 to 14 consisted of tapes that had songs missing their first ten seconds and whose final ten seconds had DJ chatter on them; from 14 to 18, I taped off my friends; from 18 to 22 I reviewed music so I could get it for free. And then after that, once I had money, I bought my music. Because I could. As for books, I bought second-hand paperbacks through my teen and college years. Now I buy hardbacks. Again, because I can. Now, being a writer, you can argue that I'm more self-interested in paying for creative work than others, but I have to honestly say that I don't know anyone who *can* pay for a book or a CD or a DVD or whatever who *doesn't*, far more often than not.

I don't see the people who can't pay as pirates. I see them as people who *will* pay, once they can. Until then, I think of it as I'm floating them a loan. Nor is it an entirely selfless act. I'm cultivating a reader—someone who thinks of books as a legitimate form of entertainment—and since I want to be a writer until I croak, that's a good investment for me. More specifically, I'm cultivating a reader of *me*, someone who will at some point in the future see a book of mine on the shelf, go "Scalzi! I love that dude!" and then take the book *off* the shelf and take it to the register.

Yes, there's an investment risk—the cash-strapped reader might in fact turn out to be a full-bore dickhead, in which case we already know what I think should happen to him—but it's a chance I'm willing to take.

It's a chance I'm willing to take because I believe that fundamentally, most people *aren't* thieving dickheads; they're people who if they like your writing will want to support your career, so long as you don't treat them like you're a mall security guard, and they're Winona Ryder. Treat readers like they can't be trusted and there's no reason for them not to live down to your expectations. Make it clear to them that they're integral to your continued success, and they will help you succeed. Treat them like human beings, for God's sake.

Here's another reason I don't worry about piracy. As most of you who read here regularly know, I recently announced that I and Tor would give free electronic copies of *Old Man's War* to service people stationed in Afghanistan and Iraq. I took the *very* minimal precaution of asking that deployed soldiers make their request from the ".mil" e-mail addresses, but other than that, I simply asked people who are not "over there" not to request a book.

It worked: I haven't gotten people misrepresenting themselves for a free book, and I haven't found one of those "over there" editions floating around aimlessly on the Web. I treated people like they were honorable adults, and so far it's worked. Until it becomes clear to me that it's not working anymore, I'll keep doing what I'm doing. If SFWA persists in wasting its time fighting an overblown battle with piracy on Amazon, it'll do it without me. It's not a battle I see worth fighting.

SELLING BOOKS
NOW

(May 17, 2005)

I'm finding the aftermath commentary to the Stupidity of Worrying About Online Piracy very interesting; apparently this subject is something people are thinking about, particularly for its long-term implications, much of which boils down to: Being willing to not worry about online piracy may work now, today, in 2005, when people are still lugging around those laughably obsolete objects known as "books." But what happens in a couple of years when the literary equivalent of the iPod hits the market, and physical books become a thing of the past, and the only copies of everything are digital—and some pirate has your entire canon of work uploaded in the P2P networks? How will you make money then? You won't be so happy about all that piracy then, will you? Where is your God now, Mr. I-Don't-Worry-About-Piracy monkey boy? Huh? Huh? Huh?

You know, these are all really *fascinating* questions, and I'm sure at the next WorldCon or other science fiction convention I'm at I'll be on a panel discussing these things with other folks, and we'll all be very interesting and thought-provoking on the matter, and who knows, maybe something we say *won't* be completely full of crap. However—and I want to be very clear on this, so allow me to use some profanity to bring the point home—in a very real and fundamental sense, *I don't fucking care.* Right now, it's 2005, I've got one science fiction book published and two more coming in the next twelve months, and my primary concern is selling those books in the here and now. *Today* I am looking for ways to get my writing in front of people, perchance to convince these fine people to purchase that writing.

Pursuant to that, the following data points.

1. *Old Man's War* has been out for six months and despite what I am told are very positive sales for a first-time unknown writer, not *once* has it been available at my local bookstore, whose science fiction/fantasy section is jammed into a corner of the store as it is, well outside the main traffic pattern, and is confined to one and a half shelves, of which three-quarters of one shelf is reserved for Star Wars/Star Trek/Tolkien crap. This one bookstore serves its town, and the towns directly north and south of it. So effectively, my book is not physically available anywhere in a 30-mile radius from my home—except at my local library, to which I donated a copy. Yes, I live in rural America, but not everything in that 30-mile radius is rural.

2. Anecdotally, I hear my book is hard to find in bookstores, period. This is partly a reflection of its strong sales (i.e., when it *is* in a bookstore, it doesn't stay long) and partly (I suspect) a reflection of Tor's printing strategy for the book, which has been of multiple small printings (the largest being the first printing of 3,800 copies), that keep Tor from having an overprint situation for a new, untested author. (Which is to say you probably shouldn't count on finding the hardcover of *Old Man's War* on the remainder table. Sorry.) I can't and don't fault Tor's logic here—the last thing I want as a new author is my publisher having rather more copies of the book than it can sell—but the regrettable side effect of this is that people can't browse a book that's not on the bookstore shelves.

3. The Kroger supermarket nearest me, whose (actually fairly extensive) book section functions as the bookstore for its town, not only doesn't stock my book, it doesn't stock science fiction at all, and aside from *Harry Potter* and *Eragon* (good job Christopher Paolini!), no fantasy, either. Not stocking my book is entirely not surprising (remember: first-time unknown SF writer in hardback), but not stocking any science fiction or fantasy *at all?* What the hell? For comparison, the store is generously stocked with romances, contemporary thillers, and westerns. Yes, westerns. You thought that genre was dead, didn't you. Surprise! The Wal-Mart and Meijer near me have remarkably similar stocking patterns.

What do these data points tell me? Clearly, that I shouldn't expect people to discover my book in the conventional ways, because *the book isn't there.* Now, some or all of these issues may be alleviated when the book goes to softcover; the reason Tor bought the book, as I've noted before, was that it believes that this is the sort of book that can crack the "no SF in supermarkets" barrier, because—yes, we can admit it here among friends—it's a Heinlein-esque adventure without all that scary edgy stuff, and maybe you can shove *that* next to the Clancys and the Grishams and sell it. If it were a car, it'd be a Chevy, and I see a fair amount of Cheveys in the Kroger parking lot. So we'll see. But that's tomorrow, and this is today.

In terms of promotion, well, I would love to promote *Old Man's War* in the Old School ways. I'm not a snob, and I'm not stupid—there's an incredible amount of promotional power in "old media." Way back when, when I met my editor at Tor for the first time, he asked me if there were any media I thought the publicity department should approach for the book. You know the first place I suggested? AARP Magazine. Because the book's about an older American, and the magazine has a subscriber roll of 21 million. It doesn't get much more old school than AARP Magazine, and I'd be a friggin' moron *not* to put the book in front of that audience. I *still* want to, hint, hint, Tor publicity department. But again: new writer, writing science fiction. I have been absolutely blessed with reviews in the *Washington Post,* in the *Cleveland Plain-Dealer* and in *Entertainment Weekly,* and it's a minor miracle I got those (not withstanding *AARP Magazine,* Tor's publicity folks rock). Most science fiction writers, even the established ones—and even the *good* established ones—would be happy with that. Right now, this is what I have to work with in terms of the Old School presence.

New School, I have options. I have this Web site, which pulls down some nice visitor numbers; I have the AOL Journal, which does the same. I have had good press from prominent bloggers, whose recommendations have translated into real sales with alacrity, because their readers trust their recommendations. Right now, there is no downside in letting someone go onto Amazon and reading as much of the book as Amazon lets them—they *are* on Amazon, after all, and one does typically go to the Amazon site to buy things. The chances of turning a sale there are good, and inasmuch as we've already established looking at a physical copy is difficult, this is the next best thing. There is no downside in offering an entire novel's worth of writing for free on my own site, as I do with *Agent to the Stars;* why *not* let people get a feel for my style? If you like *Agent* chances are pretty good you'll like *Old Man's War;* it's a different set-up and story, but, well, I'm *me,* and for better or worse, that's how I write.

Will these methods work in the future? Don't know. And, mostly, don't care, because they're working *now,* and now is the timeframe I need to sell my book in. I don't doubt that a dozen years from now, getting my books out to readers—and making money from them—will require different things and take on a different form than it does now, since among other things most of the ways I'm promoting my books now didn't exist a dozen years ago. But here are a couple things I expect to be true in 2017: that people will still want to be amused by creative types, and that the more enterprising members of that class will have found new and exciting ways of extracting money out of people who wish to be entertained. So long as I'm not dead or somehow deeply mentally damaged between now and 2017, I expect to be in the latter camp. I guess we'll find out. In the meantime, I'm happy to do what works.

WRITING
IN THE AGE
OF PIRACY

(May 19, 2005)

I came across a comment from a writer recently—which writer and where I found it I won't tell you, for reasons that will become clear shortly. It regards the nature of humans, and the business of selling books, and of piracy. To paraphrase, it said that the writer felt that the mass-market print publishing paradigm was doomed because of the online world, that 99% of customers (his estimate, not a paraphrase) are cheapskates who would pirate books if they could, and that in the future very few people would make any sort of money online, so his goal was to do everything to keep the old school publishing paradigm alive as long as possible.

My thoughts on that position?

Oh, for *fuck's* sake.

Let's translate that metaphorically, shall we? Book publishing is a sinking ship. The former passengers on the ship have given in to their feral instincts and are dismantling the ship board by board. The remaining crew are being wedged further and further back into what little of the ship remains above the waterline. Eventually the whole ship will disappear beneath the waves and all the crew will drown. The thought of possibly jumping off the ship apparently doesn't occur to the crew; rather, their ambition is simply to be *the last person to drown.*

Screw 'em. Let them drown. Because here's the thing about that "sinking ship": Even if we grant it is sinking (which we should not), and that the passengers are scurvy pirates (which we ought not), this ship is sinking in about five feet of water and the shore is fifty yards away. And if you haven't the wit to make it to shore, then by God, *you deserve to die.*

For now, let's put aside the issue of whether publishing will survive as an industry. I think it will for a number of reasons, not the least of which is that the people I've met in publishing are fairly adept capitalists who would prefer that their next gig does not involve asking people if they want fries with that. Nor do I think most people are thieving dickheads, despite the number of people recently trying to convince me otherwise. But for the sake of argument, let us posit the nuclear option: Rampant digital piracy has made it impossible to sell books. The *entire publishing industry* is out on the street. Editors are on the corners with signs that say "WILL EDIT YOUR 'WILL WORK FOR FOOD' SIGN FOR FOOD." Art directors sit on crates drawing wee little dune buggy caricatures of passersby. Publishers have launched themselves from the windows of their corner offices to publish themselves on the pavement in splattery limited editions of one. And where are the writers? If they have any sense at all, they're making a fair amount of money.

Listen to me now: **Writers are not in the publishing industry.** The publishing industry exists to handle the *output* of writers and distribute it in an effective and hopefully profitable way; however it does not necessarily follow that a writer's *only* option is the publishing industry, especially not now. Congruent to this: **Books aren't the only option.** I write books, but you know what? I'm not a book writer, any more than a musician is an LP musician or an MP3 musician. The book is the container. It's not *destiny.*

And this is where the schism exists among writers: Those who get these concepts, and those who don't. Those who don't are dead meat anyway; let's thank them for their service to letters and shed a tear as their corpses rot (and not just because of the smell). As for those of us still standing, let me introduce you to what could be your next business model.

Meet Penny Arcade (http://penny-arcade.com). Many of you already know it, of course. For those of you who don't, here's the concept: Two guys write a thrice-weekly comic strip about video games—a strip which, as it happens, is usually damn funny (often even if you don't like video games). How much money do these guys make off the strip itself? Not a dime, as far as I can tell. But the comic strip draws hundreds of thousands of visitors to the site; the site sells advertising for a fair amount every week. They sell merchandise, from t-shirts to limited edition artwork (a recent artwork sale sold 500 art "cells" at $80 a pop in less than 12 hours: $40,000 gross for 12 hours isn't bad). They have their own convention. They even have their own charity, Child's Play, which in two years has raised half a million dollars in cash and goods for children's hospitals across the country. And most importantly for the purposes of our discussion, this is their full time gig—it supports the two of them, their wives and families, and even a business manager to handle the stuff them creative types don't want to both with.

Yeah, you say, but that's a *comic strip*. I'm talking about *writing*, here. Well, listen up, funcakes: The point here is not the comic strip. The point here is what it's used for: As the basis of several different revenue streams, all of which flow directly to the principals. What happens if the cartoon strip is pirated? Not much—it's distributed for free, anyway. At the very worst, it becomes free advertising, bringing people around to the site. People visit the site; they enjoy it, they come back. That allows PA to sell advertising. Some become fans; this allows PA to sell merchandise. Some make it part of their lives; this allows PA to host a convention and fund a charity. What is at the heart of this business model is *pirate-proof content:* You can't steal free content. And what Penny Arcade sells, it's difficult to steal.

Can writers do the same thing? Well, in a universe where piracy kills the conventional publishing model, they damn well better get *used* to the idea, hadn't they.

Personally, I find this formulation non-controversial because to a very large extent it's what I do now. I won't get into how much of my writing income over the last four years comes directly and indirectly as a result of writing on my Web site, except to say it's six figures and the leftmost number is not a "1," and not nearly all of it comes from book sales. This is not bragging (or not *only* bragging, shall I say); the point to made here is that an ambitious writer can use a non-commercial presence to generate a non-trivial amount of income. In my case, the content here, like the content on Penny Arcade, is un-pirateable; I don't charge anything for it, and I don't care if you send it along to whomever you like. But it brings in thousands of people every day, some of whom would probably spend money on Scalzi merchandise. Like, say, a novel, however it is published.

Or *not* a novel, actually—why not a novella? The market for novellas is *very* small right about now, because most publishers don't like them; they don't fit into the mass-market publishing paradigm very well at all. But if I don't have to worry about my publisher's production albegra, maybe I could sell one. Or not sell it at all—maybe I'll post it up on the site with its run subsidized by an advertiser. I have eight to ten thousand visitors on a daily basis; think there's an advertiser out there who might be willing to shell out for 100,000 ad impressions over the run of the novella?

Point is, in a pirate age, I think I still stand a good chance of continuing to make a very good income from writing. Since I *don't* think we'll get to a pirate age, this is even better news for me, because I have the advantage of generating writer income the old-fashioned way as well as in this new way. Multiple revenue streams are a writer's friend. Now, get this: I'm not particularly clever, and I'm awfully lazy. If I can do this, pretty much any writer can. Yes, it does take time and effort to generate a readership (seven years, in the case of the Whatever). Tell me how this is different from publishing today.

What if I'm wrong? Well, what if I am? It's axiomatic that new formulations for generating writing income will arrive in our theoretical age of piracy; writers are creative people, and they also like to eat. I'm offering *one* potential business model here, mostly because I'm familiar with it and I know it works for me (and for Penny Arcade). If you don't like it, make one of your own. Or, you know, drown. One less writer for me to worry about.

No, these new business models are not going to work for everyone. Guess what: The publishing model *now* doesn't work for everyone, either. And guess what else: The group of Writers Making Money in the Pirate Age will not be the same as the group of Writers Making Money in the Age of Publishing. Why? Because some people *can't* do it, and some people *won't* do it. Furthermore, some people will make less money in this new age of piracy. But guess what again?

Some people will make *more,* too. Will the *per capita* income be as great? Doubtful, since this pirate age model will encourage more people whose writing would have been laughed out the door in the publishing age to make a go at monetizing their work. But I don't know how much time you need to spend worrying about the *per capita* income number. You have to worry about *your* income number.

Should you help other writers in this not entirely likely Age of Piracy? Absolutely: Karma is a good thing. Heck, you should help other writers *today.* But if all a writer can do is complain about how much better it was back *then,* and looks at his audience as if it would stab him and eat him the first chance it got, well, how much *can* you do? If someone demands that he is drowning in five feet of water, all you can do is tell him to stand up and point him in the direction of the shore. You can't make him do either.

THERE IS
ALWAYS
ANOTHER WAY

(January 16, 2006)

I have a little bit of a mania for noting significant anniversaries, and right about now marks one of
them: Ten years ago I got my job offer from America
Online, and officially left print journalism for the online
world—and along the way learned an important thing
about how the world works.

Bear in mind that leaving *The Fresno Bee*, where I worked
before I went to AOL, wasn't something I had planned on.
At the time I was very happy working for the newspaper—
but then, why wouldn't I be? I was the movie critic—the
youngest pro film critic in the US—which meant that my
job consisted of watching movies and then saying clever
things about them, and then also occasionally going down
to LA and interviewing people prettier and richer than me
as they talked about their latest projects. And to boot, I had a
newspaper column where I could pretty much write about
anything I wanted. Life was good, and I recall mentioning
to a friend that I was happy enough at my job that I could
see doing it for many years.

And of course, just like in the movies, as soon as you
mention that life is good, that means something needs to

come by and sqaut one out on your life. In my case, it was one of those periodic newspaper revamps, in which people get moved about and reassigned for no particularly good apparent reason other than because sometimes editors like to redecorate, and the way they redecorate is with staff. Call it editorial feng shui. I was called into my editor's office and the two editors of the department told me that as part of their reorganization, my column was cancelled, they were going to cut back substantially on the number of movie reviews I would do, and that I would be required to do more straight-out reporting. In short, they were taking away from me the job that I loved doing, and asking me to do a job for which I didn't feel I was suited .

Was it malicious? Almost certainly not. The editors in question were good people, and I feel reasonably sure they felt that aside from any raw talents I might have had as a writer, I could use some polish in other forms of newspaper writing. This was also one of those times where the paper was trying to do more with the staff it had on hand, and the fact of the matter was that what I did was expendable—it's not as if they couldn't find movie reviews on the wire—and they could use me as a resource for doing other things. Having now been an editor (and having now spent more time in the corporate world), I can see perfectly well the logic of their decision, and also how the editors could have sincerely believed it would be to my benefit as a writer.

Be that as it may, at the time, it felt like a sucker punch to the gut, and what compounded the issue was that, whatever the logic behind the move, I was pretty sure my editors knew (or thought they knew, in any event) that there wasn't much I could do about it. Ten years ago, as now, the number of jobs available at newspapers was smaller than the number of people competing for them, and the number of really *cool* jobs, such as mine, was much smaller. Unless I was willing to quit outright—which they rightly suspected I wasn't—then there really *wasn't* much I could do about it. Even if I went looking for another newspaper job, it could take months or even years to get.

What my editors didn't know—and to be fair, what most newspaper editors didn't know at the time—was that the print world was no longer the only way people could make money writing. By early '96, I had already been online for a couple of years (my very first Web page, in fact, went up in 1994, when one still had to hand edit html and learn unix commands to upload pages), and that was enough time for me to start getting freelance writing jobs online. One of the jobs was writing a weekly finance and humor column for America Online's Personal Finance channel (I got it largely because the person in charge of that area read something I wrote online and found it amusing). Over the several months I had written it, I had gotten to know the AOL folks pretty well, and knew they thought I was a clever enough person.

So as I was driving home that night, I decided to do something completely insane. First I signed on to AOL, and sent an e-mail to one of the AOL Vice-Presidents (the one in charge of their Web programming), and asked her if she thought AOL might be interested in buying a straight-out humor column from me. The *Bee* has cut the column, you see (I explained), and I was now free to pursue other options for it. Then I sent e-mail and waited for the VP to IM me to get the whole story, which she did about five minutes later (yes, back in the day, you could get an IM from an AOL VP—in five minutes, no less).

A few minutes after this Krissy came home from her job and walked into our bedroom to find me staring at my computer with scary, scary intensity.

"What are you doing?" she asked me.

"I'm waiting for something," I said, without taking my eyes off the computer.

"What are you waiting for?" she asked, and right then, as if on cue, the VP of AOL unofficially offered me a job.

"*That*," I said, and then turned to Krissy. "What would you think about moving to Washington, DC?"

Long story short, within an hour of being told that the *Bee* was changing my job, I had lined up another job. The next day I came in to work, and my immediate editor pulled me aside and asked, with real concern, if I was okay with my new assignments. I told him, honestly enough, that I had dealt with my issues and was ready to move forward.

Three weeks later I got my formal job offer (which I accepted via IM, to keep with the whole then-cutting-edgedness of it all), and called my editors into a meeting in which I told them I was leaving. They asked if there was anything they could do to keep me; I told them that it seemed unlikely. They asked if they could ask what I was going to be making; I told them. They both blinked; it was more than either of them made. It was their first real encounter with the online world, I suspect, and the first realization that major changes were on their way.

The move from the print world to the online world, and from California to Virginia, was immensely important to me in several ways: new work challenges and frustrations, a new crop of friends, many of whom remain quite dear to me, and of course my first full immersion into the online medium, where I still spend much of my time (heck, I'm still even working for AOL, though part-time rather than full-time). I miss working on a newspaper full-time, and I miss some of the people with whom I worked with back in Fresno—remember I wasn't originally looking to leave the paper. I was happy there. But if I had to do it all over again, I'd do it again the same way. I like where I am now, and that required leaving the "nest" of my first real job.

The most important thing the move taught me was simply this: *There is always another way.* What is required is the will to confront change from without and roll with it so it becomes change from within. My job came crashing down on me, and I had a choice of accepting it or finding another way. I found another way and and took it. My editors forced change on me; I turned it around and worked to make it a change on my terms. In this particular case I was fortunate that work I had been doing had prepared the way, so I could move quickly—but even had I started from zero, with work another way would have presented itself in time.

This was an *immensely* important thing for me to learn. It's been knowledge that I've had to remember more than once over the last ten years, most notably when AOL laid me off in 1998, and Krissy and I had to decide how to deal with it. We advanced rather than retreated and found a way to make it work. It made all the difference in the world then, and it still does today.

There is always another way. Remember that when your own challenges and changes show up and try to knock you back on your ass. Maybe they *will* knock you on your ass, but it's up to you how long you stay sprawled out. That's what I learned, a decade ago. I'm happy to share it with you now.

⸻ Chapter Three: ⸻

THE SCHADENFREUDE NEEDLE IS BURIED DEEP INTO THE RED: ON WRITERS

Why, yes, this is the catty chapter. Why do you ask? Not every entry here has me thumping on a writer for doing something remarkably stupid; at least a few of these entries are just merely me talking about something interesting involving a writer. However, it's always more fun to talk about writers behaving *badly*, particularly when it's behavior that is (or should be) easily avoidable. It's not all finger-pointing and laughing, mind you. There but for the grace of God and common sense go any number of writers—including yours truly—so it's best not to get too cocky. It's not like common sense is actually all that common, particularly in writers.

Also, to avoid the label of pure spite being applied to these entries, in most cases here there's a lesson to be learned, something simple and pure and true, like "don't encourage people to lie on cover letters, especially if you're a professor of English," or "pursuing your literary vendetta

189

in the pages of Salon makes you look like an asshole."
Think of these essays like those Afterschool Specials they
used to run, with wayward writers in place of the feath-
ered-haired teenagers sniffing glue or contracting VD or
whatever Very Special Problem those kids were having
to justify bumping *One Life to Live* out of its slot on a
Wednesday afternoon.

Yes, these entries are *just like that*. And if you imagine them
starring Kristy McNichol or Scott Baio, so much the better.

First up:

BOB GREENE
GETS CANNED

(September 16, 2002)

Chicago Tribune columnist Bob Greene resigned his position over the weekend because someone blabbed to the Tribune (in an anonymous e-mail, no less) that Ol' Bob had a sexual encounter with a teenage girl a decade ago (he would have been in his mid-40s at the time). He had met the girl in connection with his newspaper column. Interestingly enough, it's that last part that seems to be the smoking gun, not that she was a teenage girl and he was a middle-aged guy with what looks like a bad haircut, although all of that looks bad enough. Apparently she was the age of consent, even if she was a teenager (there's a couple of years where those two overlap). But having sex with someone you meet in connection with a story is a no-no.

That Bob Greene *would* have sex with a teenager while he was huffin' and puffin' away at middle age is not much of a surprise. First off, he's a guy, and if the average 40+ guy gets a chance to boink an 18-year-old without penalty (or in this case, a penalty delayed by several years), he's going to take it. Undoubtedly he'll have a good rationalization (we always do, and Greene, being a writer, probably has a better one than most), but to cut to the chase, he'll do it because she's hot and young, and because during middle age the Veil of Male Self-Deception, even at maximum power, can no longer hide the fact that one day the man will die, and that between now and then, the number of truly hot young women he can have without paying for them is small and getting smaller, fast. So that's reason number one.

Reason number two that it's not at all surprising is that Bob Greene is, by self-appointment, Boomer America's Newspaper Columnist. Well, was. Anyway, as a chronicler of the Boomer Nation observing itself, it was only a matter of time. Boomers have never done anything that wasn't eventually about them; it's the funky never-ending narcissism thing they've got going. No, that doesn't make the Boomers evil—every generation has its annoying tics (my generation, for example, has a tendency to whine like kicked puppies being shown the boots that will get them in the ribs), and this is the Boomers'. Also, rather unwisely, the Boomers made a fetish of their youth when they were younger—hey, they were young, what did they know—and they're not handling the inevitable decrepitude well. Narcissism + Getting Older = Irrational Behavior, often involving younger women in ill-advised trysts. As Boomer America's Newspaper Columnist, how could Greene *not* do this? He's just staying true to his demographic.

Reason number three is that Bob Greene telegraphed the idea he'd do (or *did*, depending on the timeline) something like this a decade ago in his perfectly awful novel *All Summer Long*. The story involves three life-long high-school chums, who when confronted with the stirrings of middle-age do what all newly-middle-aged men do in mediocre quasi-autobiographical fiction written by newly-middle-aged Boomer men: take a long vacation away from their families and responsibilities to "find themselves" on America's byways. This, of course, often involves extracurricular sex with hot babes. In the case of Bob Greene's obvious

stand-in inside the novel (a nationally well-known TV
journalist named "Ben"), this means having sex with a graduate student roughly half his age. In real life, Greene diddled
with a high school student closer to a third his age, but,
speaking as a writer, one always tries to make oneself look
better in fiction.

Now, Greene didn't *have* to follow through on the whole
sex-with-a-much-younger woman thing just because he
wrote about it. Mystery writers write about killing people
all the time; most of them don't actually attempt to follow
through. But sex with a younger woman won't kill you (just
your career) and anyway let's revisit points one and two
here. It wasn't inevitable, but when a guy draws himself a
roadmap and hands himself the keys to the car, it's not
entirely surprising he ends up in Whoops-I-slept-with-
someone-my-daughter's-age-ville, looking for a motel that
rents by the hour.

Be all that as it may, I do have to wonder what the problem
is here. Greene's sleeping with a teenage woman is gross to
think about, but they were both of legal age, and even if she
was just barely so, "just barely so," counts as legal. So far
as I know, Greene applied no coercion other than his not-
especially-dazzling celebrity, and as everyone knows, if a
great many celebrities didn't do that (especially the not-
especially-dazzling ones, and especially ones, like Greene,
who have a face for radio) they wouldn't get any action at
all; they're just as lumpy and furtive as the rest of us.

Journalistically speaking, having sex with someone in one
of your stories isn't very smart and is definitely suspension-
worthy (a nice long "leave of absence" would have been
good), but it's not a crime. From what I can tell, Greene
even waited until after he had written about the woman to
hit her up. The *Tribune* is labeling it a "breach of trust"

between journalist and subject, but if he did in fact wait until after he had written about her (and did not write about her post-boinkage), where is the breach? What I see is simply middle-age-death-denying sex, which God knows is common enough. Unseemly, sad and more than a little creepy, but there are worse things a journalist can do. Hell, it's not *plagiarism*.

There's probably more here than what we know now, that's my only guess. It's worth noting that the *Trib* didn't fire Greene; he apparently offered to resign and the resignation was accepted. If I were a corporate suit, I'd've taken the resignation too, since it was an easy way to distance my company from Greene's compromising position.

Also, I think Greene should have been cut as a columnist years ago, not because he's morally tainted, but because he's a boring columnist. He stopped being interesting and started being filler long before he did his questionable after-school activities. From a purely utilitarian point of view, there's no downside to Greene hightailing it out of town, excepting that there will be the painfully rationalized *mea culpa* six months down the road as part of Greene's inevitable comeback (America loves a reformed sinner).

But based on what we know now, this isn't the way Greene should go out. If he needed to be yanked, he should have been yanked on the merits of his writing (or lack thereof), not because of sex he had a decade ago with a legal adult who apparently gave her consent after she was no longer his journalistic subject. Greene is getting popped on a dubious technicality, and though I would have never imagined I'd say something like this, I think he probably deserves better. Getting canned for being a boring columnist would probably have been harder on the ego, but at least it would have been a reasonable excuse for getting escorted from the building. I won't much miss Greene's columns, but even I wish he could have had a better final act.

BOB GREENE
REDUX

(September 18, 2002)

Interesting feedback from the Bob Greene thing the other day. Aside from the journalistic schadenfreude of watching Bob Greene fall—which is considerable, so that's a warning to all of you who wish you had his career up until last weekend—the largest spate of e-mail I got about it came from 40-plus-year-old men who wanted me to know that they don't like 18-year-old girls. Not at all. My universal response to these fellows was: Good for you. I'm sure your wives are proud.

As it happens, I'm not so keen on 18-year-olds myself; in the grand scheme of things, procuring one today would be more trouble than it's worth. This has nothing to do with their physical charms (about which I'll comment in a minute) and pretty much everything to do with the fact that at the age of 33, the only two things I have in common with the typical 18-year-old girl are that we are both human and speak the same language, plus or minus a couple dozen words of slang. To be terribly male about it, I suppose I *could* have sex with an 18-year-old if I *had* to. I just wouldn't enjoy the post-coital conversation very much. So if it's all the same I'll pass. Fortunately for me, there are not great throngs of 18-year-old hotties at my door, licking the window panes to entice me to let them come up for a romp. You can imagine my relief.

Over at Slate, Mickey Kaus begs to differ about my point concerning Greene's encroaching mortality being a consideration for his boinking a teenage woman; Kaus writes:

> "Why do men—like Scalzi here, or Warren Beatty in Shampoo (or whoever wrote Warren Beatty's lines in Shampoo)—have to explain their desire to have sex with attractive women in terms of a struggle against mortality ("middle-age-death-denying" in Scalzi's words)? You mean they wouldn't have sex with young women if they were in good shape and knew they were going to live to be 300? They didn't want to have sex with young women when they were young themselves? It's sex! Millions of years of evolution have designed men to want it and enjoy it.. It's stupid to try to explain this urge in some highfalutin' literary or spiritual way—and revealing that even relatively no-BS men like Scalzi (or Nick Hornby in High Fidelity, to name another) feel that they have to."

Let's separate this out. There's the first point, on which Kaus is entirely correct, which is that boinking hot young women is really its own excuse. You all know the drill concerning the genetic and cultural reasons for this, so let's pretend I've made all those points so we can move on. There is the point to be made here that (some) men are turned off by the yawning chasm in life experience between themselves and the average 18-year-old, and therefore prefer the company of women nearer their own age. As I mentioned earlier: Good for them.

On the other hand: Provide a man with the brain of a 45-year-old woman (yes, he'll suddenly become smarter, ha ha ha, thank you very much) and tell him he can put it either into the body of a fit, attractive 45-year-old woman, or into the body of a fit, attractive 18-year-old woman. Let's all not pretend that the 45-year-old body is going to do anything but sit there with a blinking neon "vacancy" sign flashing over its head. In a perfect world (for men) women would hover around age 23 forever (In a perfect world for women, I expect you'd see a lot more variation in age, from a Heath Ledger 22 to a Pierce Brosnan 49, with the median being a Brad Pitt 38).

Still, conceding this point, which I readily do, doesn't mean that middle-age dudes still don't actually see (or at least rationalize) porking the young as a fist in the snout of death. It's not especially highfalutin' to point it out, it's actually pretty sad and common. If you're thinking about death, or how you've squandered your potential in middle management or wherever, you want to do things that make you feel alive. Having sex with young women is the male mid-life crisis version of the Make-A-Wish Foundation. It doesn't keep you from dying, but at least you get to go to the Magic Kingdom one more time.

Whether this is the particular case with Bob Greene is another matter entirely. As journalist Nancy Nall notes on her site, Greene has had a reputation as a skirt-chaser for a while now, so if these scandalous rumors are true, he's merely pursuing a *modus operandi* honed over decades (*eeeeew*). In which case Kaus carries the day. This encounter really is less about middle-aged angst than it is just about making a fast and easy booty call on the Youth of America: Dinner and dessert. Let's hope it was at least an expensive dinner. Taking the girl out to Harold's Chicken Shack before slipping her the drumstick would just be chintzy and sad.

ATTACK OF THE MONKEYFISHERS

(June 26, 2001)

Oops. After spending about a week defending author Jay Forman's article on the dubious sport of "Monkeyfishing" (in which Forman alleges to have witnessed live monkeys hooked on a fishing pole through the use of apples and a strong fishing line), Slate rather shamefacedly had to admit that the relevant facts of the article (i.e., the trip to fish for monkeys and the subsequent sordid details) were made up, and apologized for the whole affair. Apparently, no animals were harmed in the creation of the article after all.

I'm a little surprised about the apology, and not simply because *Slate* is an arm of Microsoft, whose *modus operandi* is never to apologize about anything, from monopolistic practices and pathetically shoddy 1.0 products, to that whole painful "Bob" thing several years back (although to Microsoft's credit, it does seem to be going out of its way to publicly disavow Clippy, the irritating paper clip "helpbot" with the disturbingly unattached eyeballs). I'm surprised because I can't believe that anyone ever thought that the "Monkeyfishing" article was anything *but* fiction in the first place.

"Monkeyfishing" was one in a series of articles that Forman wrote for *Slate* under the rubric of "Vices." Other articles (at least one more of which, incidentally, features fabricated or inaccurate details) had Forman shootin' guns while tanked and working in the porn industry, writing steamy "letters to the editor" a la *Penthouse Forum*. These articles were entertaining as hell to read, so at the very least *Slate* can say that its liars give good value. The articles are also wildly out of place at *Slate*, whose editorial voice lacks the sort of raggedly breathless edge that *Salon* has made famous; indeed, Forman's columns were positively *Salon*-esque (which probably should have tipped someone off right there).

But it's also clear in the reading that Forman's personal life is a little *too* interesting. Sure, *any* of us could unload a clip while drunk, or write punchy one-fisted prose, or wrestle a feisty rhesus monkey into a net. However, with the arguable exception of Hunter Thompson, not a one of us could do *all* of these things in one lifetime. The karmic load is too great to bear. We'd devolve into millipedes without having to die and come back first. In any event, Forman's take on things was perhaps a little too observational given the circumstances; the finely-filigreed descriptions of shootin' while splotzed out on Jaegermeister, for example, bespeak an eye for detail rather too undimmed for that particular drinkable, which is notorious for unscrewing one's optic nerves faster than anything short of actual antifreeze.

My honest assumption, after having read the first of these articles (the one about drinkin' and shootin'), was that Forman was hired not for his skills at *reportage*, but to write up some barely plausible fictions that would get *Slate* readers hopped up and arguing, and have them sending the article to similarly morally outraged friends; i.e., a classic circulation-boosting move. The "Monkeyfishing" article is a laudable example of this form: start with a liberal-enraging concept (hooking primates! Why, they're very nearly hominids!), bait the hook—so to speak—with some plausible details, like how the monkeys were in the Florida swamps because of an abandoned scientific experiment, and then get things revved up with a recounting of an actual expedition, with just a smidgen of humanity thrown in (the "catch and release" idea) to make the essay go down smooth.

Heck, it's just like Swift's "A Modest Proposal," except that where Swift was railing against the severe economic and social injustices in British-suppressed Ireland, Forman is sheepishly declaring that taunting monkeys with a fishing line is, like, totally *not* cool, a rather lower target to hit (and hopefully something most of us could have figured out on our own). In either case, however, the details are not the point, whether they consist of Americans eating babies or Americans fishing monkeys. The point is to get the audience both uncomfortable and engaged. Forman ain't Swift (nor all that swift, since he got caught), but he certainly achieved the objective of stirring up the animals, to use H.L. Mencken's colorful and in this case contextually apt phrase.

To discover now that the folks over at *Slate* actually believed these gonzo adventures were true makes me feel a little sad and embarrassed for them. It's one thing to present a story about a monkey on a hook; it's another thing to find out that you're that monkey's uncle. On the other hand, I have a good idea what subject Forman could write about for his next "Vice" column. Assuming the *Slate* folks will ever let him write for them again. Which of course they will not.

Forman's acts of fiction will strike most folks as incredibly stupid. After all, here's a guy with a semi-regular gig at one of the few remaining online sites that **a)** actually pays, and **b)** is not in danger of evaporating in a spasm of choked-off VC funding (it pays to be a province of the Microsoft Empire), and he screws it up by making crap up. Not only that, but he also screws himself out of future writing gigs, since no editor with his brain switched on is going to let him anywhere near his publication. So the question is, what drives an otherwise (let's assume) perfectly sane human being to willfully mess up a sweet deal? I've got a few ideas:

a) Desperation—Let's face it, it can't be easy being any publication's "vice" columnist, since it requires a lifestyle that includes a high risk of communicable diseases, chronic misdemeanor arrests, liver damage and court-mandated encounter sessions with fellow addicts. Also, most people are fundamentally boring—it takes genuine effort to go out and pick up vices. I suspect Forman simply couldn't keep up with the lifestyle the column presumed, and had to make stuff up to keep his editors happy. One can imagine the sort of editorial notes he'd be getting:

> *Jay: This article looks fine, but I think it needs a splash more sodomy to really get going. Jam some in, would you? There's a dear—MK*

Really, who could keep up? Who would *want* to?

b) Overconfidence—Successful writers are, by necessity, total bullshit artists, and yes, I cheerfully include myself in this assessment, although I have not to this date entirely fabricated a story so far as anyone knows. The problem is when you start to believe in your own bullshit, and in your ability to serve up the same. Writing up the monkeyfishing article, Forman was probably sitting there giggling about how damned funny he was and how his article was probably going to go over big. What he probably wasn't thinking about was that checking up on the truth of his story was going to be a hell of a lot easier than he would ever assume. Any time you bullshit, you take a risk, and the longer you get away with bullshit, the more risks you inevitably take.

The moral: Writers, conserve your bullshit. Use it sparingly. And for God's sake, don't assume you can shovel a huge pile and get away with it. Bullshit stinks, and given a big enough pile, everyone can smell it.

c) Laziness/Stupidity—If there's absolutely one thing the Internet Age should teach writers, it is that you can't get away with being lazy and stupid anymore. Snip a paragraph or two out of someone else's column and slip it into your own, or make up a story that's supposed to be true but isn't, and the next thing you know, someone's written a letter to MediaNews.org outing your screw-up, and you're out on your ass. Journalists, bless our black little hearts, are petty and vindictive and love to flog our hallowed journalism ethics whenever there's some momentary advantage and/or amusement value in doing so. You will get caught because other journalists are trained to investigate and they love to turn on their own. And they're not entirely wrong to do it, either. Stupidity is no good for the rest of us.

d) Creative Constipation—Work with me here. **Thesis:** There is no real market for fiction any more. Get outside of the *New Yorker* and *Playboy*, and basically you have to publish your fiction in podunk literary journals that pay you in copies. **Antithesis:** Every writer has a novel or a bunch of short stories festering inside (trust me). **Synthesis:** Lacking a viable outlet for fiction, certain writers will get a little too creative with their non-fiction. Call me crazy for floating this one, but look, as a writer sometimes you just want to make stuff up. *And* get paid for it.

Would Jay Forman still be writing for *Slate* if he could have just managed to sell a little fiction on the side—a story about a wacky monkeyfishing expedition, perhaps? We'll never know, but I think it's worth finding out. Maybe *Slate* should start publishing fiction every now and again. Intentionally, I mean.

STINKY CHEESE

(September 20, 2002)

Krissy came home the other night with *Who Moved My Cheese?* It was pressed onto her at work by one of the managers at her new place of employment, who told her that all new hires were actively encouraged to read it (Here's a clue to the sensible Midwestern frugality of her new place of work: rather than buying a copy for every new hire, which would cost $20 a pop at list price, they simply lend out the same copy over and over). My understanding is that it's arguably the number one business motivational book on the market. Well, I'm in business, and I prefer to be motivated, so I read it. And now I can say, if this is what people are using to motivate themselves in corporate America today, no wonder the Dow is where it's at. It is, without exception, the stupidest book I have ever read.

The motivational lessons in the book come in the form of a parable, suitable for reading to your three-year-old, about four creatures in a lab-rat maze. Two of them are mice, and two of them are little mice-size humans, and they eat the cheese that's placed in a certain location in the maze. Eventually, the amount of cheese decreases and then disappears. The mice, who noticed the decreasing amounts of cheese, take off through the maze to find more cheese. The little humans, on the other hand, bitch about the loss of cheese and reminisce about the days when cheese was plentiful. Eventually one of the humans gets off his ass and heads out to find more cheese, and in doing so, has a motivational epiphany every few steps, which he feels compelled to scrawl on the walls of the maze.

Eventually he finds more cheese in the maze, as well as the mice, who have grown fat and happy with their new store of food. The little human considers going back for his friend, but then decides that, no, his friend must find his own way through the maze. He leaves his old pal to starve, as that's almost certainly what his dim, stubborn friend does, and feels all shiny and self-important for finding his new cheese.

The entire parable is framed with a conversation between several friends, one of whom is telling the parable, and the rest of whom spend the parable's epilogue wondering how they ever got through their professional and personal lives without hearing about the cheese (an interesting rhetorical cheat, incidentally—the author is confirming the usefulness of the book by creating characters that are helped by its philosophy, but which don't actually exist in the real world. This is a very Ayn Rand thing to do).

The overall idea of the book is that change is inevitable and if you're smart, when it happens you won't spend much of your time bitching about how you don't like change; instead you'll adapt to the change and get on with your life. The "cheese" represents all the things you've come to rely upon. Well, let me save you 20 bucks and boil the lesson of the book down to exactly five words: *Shit Happens. Deal With It.*

Also, the book throws in a few other lessons, which are hopefully unintended:

1. Life is a maze that has been laid out without your control or consent. The best you can do is run through it and hope you run into the things that make you happy.

2. You have no control over the things that make you happy—their quantity and quality are controlled totally by outside forces, with whom you cannot interact, and which have no interest in your needs.

3. The mice in the parable understood that the "cheese" was decreasing but neither informed the little humans nor seemed interested in helping them once the cheese was gone. Mice represent the "other." You cannot trust the "other." Stick to your own kind (alternately, the mice represent management, who know more about the reality of the situation, and the little humans are the rank-and-file, intentionally kept in the dark by management. Either way: Not to be trusted).

4. The one little human found more cheese but decided not to return to help his friend, rationalizing that it was up to his friend to find the way. Moral: Once you've got yours, you don't need to share. It's not your responsibility to share your knowledge with others, even if the cost of sharing that knowledge is trivial and doing so will immeasurably improve their lives (i.e., in this case, keep the other little human from starving to death).

In other words, the formulation of the book posits a world that is confusing and sterile, in which the things that might make us happy all exist outside of ourselves, and in which the ultimate successful qualities are selfishness and paranoia. I wonder how popular this book was at Enron and Global Crossing.

Look, people. If you ever find your "cheese" decreasing, don't run around frantically in a maze, looking for something else to replace it. Simply learn to make cheese. Which is to say, be responsible for creating your own happiness internally instead of relying on something outside of you to provide it, and living in fear that it will go away. This way, when the cosmic forces take away your cheese, you can look up and say, *screw you and your stinkin' maze. I'll move when I damn well feel like it.*

Even better, you won't have to compete with others for your cheese. Heck, eventually you'll have surplus cheese to give to your friends who might be starving for some. You can teach them to make cheese, too. Give a man a piece of cheese, and he has cheese toast for a day. Teach him how to make cheese, and you've got a life-long fondue party pal.

Mmmm. Fondue. Much better than scampering blindly through a maze. Or paying $20 for a book that condescendingly tells you that's what you should be doing with your life.

BEING AN
E-AUTHOR

(July 31, 2001)

Author MJ Rose wrote a fairly interesting article yesterday about being known as an "e-author"—Rose
self-published her first novel online and generated enough
buzz to have it picked up by a traditional publisher, and has
since written two other books that have been traditionally
published. However, the traditional books (and her career
as a novelist) have taken a back seat to her being known as
"the e-book woman"—a circumstance that apparently causes
other published writers to sneer while making her a magnet
to wanna-be writers, for whom being e-published is a step
up from what they are now, which is nothing (in terms of
being authors). In short, Rose is known for what she's done
rather than what's she's written, which is not really what an
author wants.

In a sense I understand where she's coming from,
since I have one book out in the stores and a novel which
(like her), I self-published on my Web site. However,
unlike her, when I meet other writers or people ask what
I've written, I lead with the published book and rarely if
ever mention the novel at all, precisely because it is on
Web and not in a bound book. As Rose communicates in the
article, tell someone you've published on the Web and
immediately a sign goes up over your head which blinks

"NOT A REAL AUTHOR" in bright pink neon. Better not to bring it up at all. It's sad for the novel, of course, which is a decent enough read and which is on the Web at least partly due to by own laziness (it was easier to put it up than flog it for years at various science fiction publishers), but I accept it as part of the territory.

The reason why Rose gets no respect for being e-published and why I don't bring up my novel is simply this: Because most "books" on the Web well and truly suck. Self-published "books," of course, are generally the sludge of the whole Web barrel—dreck so bad that not even e-publishers will touch them. From time to time I'll go and check out a self-published novel on the Web. It's rare I get past the first page, and sometimes it's a challenge to get past the first paragraph, which as often as not is one tremendous run-on sentence. Yes, James Joyce has a whole chapter in "Ulysses" that is one long run-on sentence. However **a)** someone paid Joyce for "Ulysses," and **b)** these people on the Web ain't Joyce.

Beyond the self-published dreck are the e-publishers, who also publish a whole lot of dreck, although it's not entirely their fault. Simply put, e-publishers don't get first crack at the good stuff—every writer who is worth a damn hits traditional publishers first (if for no other reason than that their agents wouldn't be caught dead shilling their clients to e-publishers unless they absolutely had to; it's bad for business). By the time a work filters down to the e-publishers, it's usually for a reason, that being that it couldn't be sold anywhere else. It's sort of like how actors are in B-movies not because they *want* to be, but because they don't have any *choice*. E-publishing is the straight-to-video of the literary world.

(Let us stipulate at this point that yes, indeed, traditional publishers spew out astounding amounts of dreck as well.

Anyone who attempts to read any sort of genre fiction knows this to be true. However, traditionally published dreck is typically a better class of dreck than e-published dreck, and certainly exponentially better than self-published-on-the-Web dreck.)

Not all e-published work is crap, of course. Some of it is very good (and if you're an e-author who is reading this, I'm sure *your* e-book is the finest e-book ever published). That's not my point. My point is, regardless of the quality of the best of e-published books and novels, the general quality range of e-published work, and the fact it's always the "second-best" publishing option, will always conspire to denigrate anyone who publishes in this medium. And I doubt this will change, until technology changes enough to erase all the practical differences between e-publishing and traditional publishing. This would require an e-book reader that is as easy to read as a traditional book, durable to abuse as much as we abuse paperbacks and cheap enough that when you lose it, you can buy another one without wincing at the dent in your wallet. Technology is an amazing thing, but we're still a long way off from that.

(The other option is to have e-publishers start paying exorbitant amounts to have top writers publish original works directly to digital form, but, yeah, like *that's* happening any time soon. There is an e-publisher who is reprinting modern author classics, but I expect that to flop, since the paperbacks are still out there.)

The solution to Rose's problem is simple, incidentally. If she wants to stop being known as an "e-author," she should simply stop talking and writing about it. She is a traditionally published author now; she can look at the other authors who treat her with slight regard and say, "hey, bite me, I've got three books in the stores." It's hard to argue with success.

Of course, the flip side of this is that very few magazines, newspapers or TV shows are interested in authors for what they've *written*. MJ Rose is an author known for what she's done, but she *is* known. It's publicity, no matter of what sort, and it's hard to let go of.

THE STUPIDEST CRITICISM OF A CLINTON, THIS WEEK

(June 12, 2003)

G regg Easterbrook, an ESPN2 columnist and senior editor at the *New Republic*, takes a whack at Hillary Clinton and her bookwriting prowess, presenting some interesting evidence that she's a "liar" in his column :

> *"Living History is a 562-page book. A work of that length would take an average writer perhaps four years to produce; a highly proficient writer might finish in two years, if working on nothing else. Clinton signed the contract to 'write' the book about two years ago. About the same time, she also was sworn in as a member of the United States Senate. Clinton took an oath to protect the Constitution and to serve the citizens of New York. So in the last two years Clinton has either been neglecting her duties as a United States Senator—that is, violating her oath—in order to be the true author of Living History, or she is claiming authorship of someone else's work. Considering that Clinton has made almost daily public appearances during the period when she was supposedly feverishly 'writing' her book, let's make a wild guess which explanation pertains."*

What Easterbrook ultimately appears to be wound up about is that it's probably *very* likely Clinton used a ghost-writer for some or all of the book and yet she's taking all of the credit. Well, this is a stupid argument. I don't think anyone's terribly shocked that politicians and celebrities use ghostwriters for their books. It's unlikely that Easterbrook will find much traction for this outrage up on the Hill, since just about every politician up there who has published a book has used a ghostwriter for it.

And if Easterbrook wants to get exercised about Clinton, he'll also need to get exercised about JFK, whose Pulitzer Prize-winning *Profiles in Courage* was probably written by Theodore Sorenson, and Ronald Reagan, who reportedly said of his own autobiography that he had heard it was a great book and that he should read it sometime.

With politicians there's the accepted fact that their words are written for them all the time—they have speech-writers. When a president goes up and gives a State of the Union address, no one in his right mind believes that he's written that speech himself (this is particularly the case with the current resident of the White House). However, news reports don't say "Tonight, President Bush, as written by David Frum, announced sweeping new tax proposals." The words are attributed to Bush. The same thing happens with columns and articles produced by politicians for news-papers and magazines. Be that as it may, most of us accept the words as the politicians'. I don't see the nation rising up to contest this apparent theft of work. We get the concept.

Also, it's not as if ghostwriters are typically abused by the agreement. By and large, ghostwriters for prominent celebs and politicians get a hefty upfront payment and some cut of the royalties. And of course the ghostwriter him or herself is known to the publishers, which positions the writer nicely for another profitable ghostwriting assignment or for his or her own works. If Clinton used a ghostwriter, it's unlikely you'll hear the ghostwriter complain about the arrangement. By and large, it's a good deal for the writer.

(Well, this time, anyway—the ghostwriter for Clinton's *It Takes a Village* got into an argument with her about credit and complained to the media. Presumably Clinton and her publisher made it clear with whatever ghostwriter they might have used this time what the situation would be.)

Probably the best way to look at the ghostwritten works of politicians and celebrities is to approach them like you would "solo" albums by musicians. Solo albums are anything but—usually there are songwriters, producers, engineers and other musicians who contribute to the effort. When you think about solo albums by celebrities, usually soap stars, the "solo" aspect of it becomes even less accurate. No one expects the singer to do every single thing on the album, unless they are Prince.

Well, you say, at least these people *sing* on their albums. True enough. But it's not as if Clinton, if she did use a ghost-writer, was totally uninvolved. First off, it *is* her story, and whatever part of the book she did not write herself, she still had direct supervision of its writing; rest assured that nothing in that book got past her without her approval. Clinton may have not scribbled out every word of it herself, but the book says exactly what she wants it to say. It's undoubtedly *her* book. She's the producer. So, I suppose, you could think of it as the literary equivalent of an Alan Parsons Project album.

Thereby, I don't think it's especially dishonest of her to present it as her own, with her name solely on the cover. Easterbrook is merely being intentionally obtuse about how politicians write their books in order to take a whack at Clinton. Easterbrook mentions that some politicians include their ghostwriter's names on the cover. Sure. And some *don't*. Clinton's not the first, and she won't be the last, from either side of the aisle. And unless she specifically comes right out and says "Yes, I wrote every single word in my book with no help from anyone else whatsoever"—which I'm unaware that she has done—she's not lying.

Speaking of obtuseness on the part of Easterbrook, his comment that it would take the average writer four years to write a 562-page book is complete and total crap. In four years (1999 through 2002) I wrote three books under my own name (each about 90,000 words, or roughly 300 pages each), and contributed to another three books to the tune of about 60,000 words, or another 200 pages. Currently I'm working on two additional books, one due in September and one in October, both of which will also come out to about 90,000 words, or yet another 300 pages each.

So, in five years, I will have produced five books under my own name and contributed to three other books for a grand total of about 510,000 words and about 1,700 pages. Note this is on top of writing newspaper and magazine columns and articles, corporate writing assignments and writing untold thousands of words here on this site. To put it simply, if I could only produce 560 pages of writing in four years, I would starve. I'm glad the "average" writer can only write that much. It means more work for me. But in fact the "average" writer can write substantially more than Easterbrook (himself an author of three books) claims—as could a working senator, I'm sure, if she put her mind to it.

No matter how you slice it, Easterbrook's moral outrage concerning Clinton's book is pretty much bogus. Either he's obtuse about how publishing works, or he's misrepresenting what he knows. I'll assume the former. I would hate to think Mr. Easterbrook has a problem with honesty.

ENVY

(July 22, 2003)

There's an interesting article by the former girlfriend of Jonathan Franzen, the now-famous writer of *The Corrections*, and of other books I haven't read but which I am told are very good (and not just because Oprah thinks so). It's mostly about her observing herself observing her ex-boyfriend's literary fame, which is a matter of personal import since she is herself a writer, and simply put, it's not usually a very good thing when the person who you are with does the same thing you do and does better (in terms of finances and fame) than you do. This is especially true of writers, who live much of their lives internally and therefore have more time (and ability of expression) to stew and envy and plot and pick.

One should never generalize about these things, but I personally think that a real good recipe for misery would be two writers in a romantic relationship with each other. Others may disagree: They may say that a spouse who writes understands what you're going through, might be able to offer perspective and guidance and assistance, and all that happy crap. But as valuable as those things might be, there's another far more detrimental dynamic, which is that unless they are writing wholly disparate things—say, one writes fiction and one writes science textbooks, and neither has the ambition to dabble in the other's area—two writers under the same roof are always competing with each other, for the cleverest lines, the most sales, for the most raw talent.

And what's more, the happy couple are competing with each other in a medium that encourages the author to digest the minutiae of personal life and disgorge it onto the page. The two authors will soon be feeding on each other for material, and if that isn't incestuous and recursive enough, when one of them becomes more successful than the other, the other will hate them for it. Not all—some writers are secure enough in what they're doing (or relish their indie cred enough) that they don't see the success of their spouse or lover as a negative commentary on their own work. I even know a couple. But, shall we say, they're remarkably secure people in a field filled with twitchy types.

One of the things that I have always been relieved about regarding my own marriage is that Krissy and I have no cause to compete on a professional level. She has no ambitions to write for a living, and I have no desire to do what she does, and that leaves the both of us to be wholeheartedly supportive of each other without even the slightest hint of envy or un-happiness. I want my wife to be madly successful, and she me. If she manages one day to become a VP or CEO, I'm not going to sit around wondering if I should be at the same place in my own career; if I write a best-selling book one day, she's not going to wonder why I was doing so well when her book of short stories was being remaindered. Marriage is work enough without having to define your success relative to your spouse.

Success is a funny thing anyway, especially for creative types. You have to train yourself not to begrudge it to others, and indeed to want others to succeed in your field. Writers are supremely passive-aggressive (again part and parcel of that whole spending too much time in your own head thing), and it's an effort not to wonder what someone else's success means for your own or your own lack thereof. Eventually you have to realize that success is not a zero-sum game (well, technically it *is*, because there's a finite number of publishers with a finite amount of resources, publishing a finite amount of books every year—but all those numbers are large enough that for the individual author, the point is moot). Despite what you may think, the success of others is not a referendum on you.

Eventually you realize there's a positive value in the success of others, especially if you know them or are connected to them in some way. I am tickled six kinds of pink that my friend Pamela Ribon's book has been flying off the shelves and that my friend Naomi Kritzer's fantasy series has been so well received. I know Cory Doctorow only through the "Six Degrees of Separation" group-hug that's known as the blog world, but I feel invested in the fine performance of his novel because it's proof that you can put your work online and people will still choose to shell out for it in traditional form. Everyone who succeeds shows that success is possible; I've also found that those who have success usually want their friends to succeed as well. I know in my own case that I can name a couple of writers who I can't wait to be "next"—I want them in the same club I'm in because I like being with my friends.

But I'll also note I'm not married to any of these people, and although I like to think of myself as genially secure in the success of these other writers, I'm also pleased not to be in a position where I have to worry about how my dealing with their success affects our mortgage and children. As I said, romantic relations are complicated enough. The possibility of envying the success of the one you love shouldn't be a part of it. I'm glad in my case it's not.

WORKSHOP
FRACAS

(July 26, 2003)

This is interesting to me: Gene Wolfe, the noted fantasy writer, was the author-in-residence at the Odyssey Fantasy Writers Workshop earlier this month. As Wolfe began his critiques, some of the members of the workshop were apparently taken aback at his style and his bluntness; after a few days of this, one of the workshop members submitted a letter to Wolfe complaining about his style. Wolfe's response to the letter was to pack up and leave. This was followed almost immediately by several participants recounting the story online, including Wolfe; it's like *Roshomon*, in workshop form.

I should note that coloring this commentary is my personal aversion to the workshop concept, which has more to do with my own personality than it does the relative value of sitting around talking about your writing with other writers. For some people it works. On my end—and this is my raging egotism here—I'd rather spend my time putting my work in front of people who are going to pay me for my work, than pay to have people read it. We can talk about the value of workshops in becoming a *better* writer, whatever that means, but being that I write for a living, I'm more interested in becoming a *commercial* writer, and unfortunately commentary on my writing from a bunch of other unpublished writers is of little utility in that regard. Being a *better* writer is something of a moot point, since if you're not a commercial writer to some extent, very few people will know whether your writing is any good or not.

But of course it works the other way, too—were I an unpublished writer, any comments I could give other writers would be of questionable utility, since my experience with being published would be minimal. I could offer my thoughts as a reader, but then, so could any literate person. So, to get back to the workshop thing, I don't see what the value is in paying a couple grand to have a bunch of readers read my work. I could get that done for free (look what you're doing right now).

Now, at this point in my life, I'd be willing to participate in a workshop environment because I'm on the other end of the stick—I've been a professional writer for 12 years, I've published (or will have published) a number of books, and I've also been a commercial editor, charged with buying and then editing submissions from writers. In other words, I now have a level of experience that means that when I make a comment or suggestion regarding the writer's work, it would have some practical, real world value. I wouldn't feel like a total ass telling an aspiring writer what I thought were the pluses and minuses of the work. This is professional pride in action: I've been around the block a few times now. I know whereof I speak. Mostly.

So, in short: Workshops—*eh*. I'd go for the pros and their comments. Everything else is group-huggy self-affirmation.

Alas for the people at the Odyssey Workshop, many of them seem to have gone for the group-huggy self-affirmation rather than the useful aspect of having their work read and commented upon by a professional—and to have the exposure to how a professional writer approaches the work, and how the professional world approaches writing as well. One of the most interesting and telling comments came from workshop participant Sarah Totten, who wrote in her journal about Odyssey, after first being exposed to Wolfe and his critical style: "Since when did writing become a competitive sport? We're supposed to be fostering camaraderie here, not cutthroat one-upmanship."

Anyone who believes professional writing is not a competitive sport needs to take a field trip to any of the major publishing houses and take a long loving look at the slush pile. Professional writing is *intensely* competitive. I'll trot out my favorite personal example here: When I was editing that humor area on America Online lo those many years ago, I had 20 open spaces a month to fill with submissions. I got, on average, 1,000 submissions a month. This means that for every piece I accepted, I rejected 49, which is (if my spotty math holds up) a 98% rejection rate. And when you consider that after the first couple of months, more than half of my available slots went to people I worked with before and knew could provide me quality material, the real world rejection rate for someone sending me something blind was 99+%. It was substantially easier to get into Harvard than to place work with me.

In fact, the sports analogy is an interestingly sound one when it comes to publishing (especially book publishing). Each major publisher is like a major league baseball team, which has a certain number of slots to fill on its playing card every year and a certain amount of money to spend to fill those slots. The all-stars are few and get the most money, and the rest of the holes are filled with utility players just happy to be in the game instead of having to lift appliances for a living (which one am I? Are you kidding? I know what I got for an advance. Right now, I'm a utility infielder all the way. I just hope I can help the team, and God willing, everything will work out).

Every year, some potentially exciting new players get picked up, some underperforming old players get dropped. Some have Hall of Fame careers. Some go back to their day jobs and are glad they at least got into The Show. Writing is a business as well as everything else it is, and if you're going to go pro, you have to perform. Someone is ready to take your place in the publisher's lineup if you don't. Competition is built in. Maybe it's not fair, but the real world isn't like t-ball, where everybody gets to bat.

As for camaraderie, I think it's a great idea: I know other writers, I like other writers. I like seeing other writers I know succeed. But ultimately it's not what professional writing's about, any more than great dugout camaraderie is the point of a professional baseball team. The Detroit Tigers could very well have the most self-affirming dugout in the major leagues, but the fans would probably rather the players hated each other's guts and won 100 games. A writer's audience cares about what's on the page; the professional writer's job is to give the readers a reason to care (and hopefully to care with their wallets and charge cards). No amount of group hugging will matter if your writing doesn't sell itself.

Ms. Lincoln, in describing her reaction to Mr. Wolfe's critique, wrote: "Wolfe's critique didn't give me anything the rest of the class couldn't deliver, only more tactfully." Ms. Lincoln, with no disrespect to her follow workshoppers, is probably wrong on this; Mr. Wolfe has published a couple dozen novels across four decades, as well as innumerable short stories over a longer span of time, many of which have been nominated for (and on several occasions have won) the various top SF/F awards. This means he has an excellent combination of overall writing skill and commercial savvy;

no one gets continuously published over four decades if he doesn't know what he's doing in both departments.

Writing skill doesn't necessarily imply teaching skill, however. But in this case Mr. Wolfe has taken part in workshops at Clarions East and West and at Florida Atlantic University, and taught creative writing at Columbia University. So all the way around, Wolfe has the personal and professional experience to provide useful criticism, in a way that the others in the workshop almost certainly could not (otherwise they wouldn't *be* there).

Wolfe's crime, as far as I can see, was to provide criticism in a manner not to the liking of the workshop members. And this is where I, both as a professional writer and as a professional critic, have to ask: So? Is it the instructor's job to be liked, or is it his job to provide useful information? When I was in high school, I remember telling one of my teachers one day that I thought his classes would go more successfully if he tried connecting with the students in a way that was more on their level.

He tried it the next day, and whether he was intentionally mocking me or merely making a sincere attempt, I couldn't say. But I can say it was probably the most deeply embarrassing experience I had as a student, in that I suggested something that was so obviously ill-suited to the man. It was also the first time I realized that teachers who don't teach us the way we think we want to be taught aren't always bad teachers. Maybe the way they teach in itself is a lesson. I can't say that I became a better student in that particular class, but I do know I paid more attention to *how* my teacher tried to teach me.

And maybe that's what Wolfe was doing, too. Wolfe's critical style was by all accounts confrontational, comparative and deeply subjective, to which I say: Welcome to criticism.

Constructive criticism doesn't have to be "nice"; it can be abrupt and offensive. Criticism can shock you out of your complacency and remind you that the world is not in fact a cozy circle of workshop buddies. I'm not Wolfe, so I can't say what he was thinking, but I do know that the real world of writing is confrontational (unless you think rejection is a passive act), comparative (in that editors always have something else in the pile to go with instead of your piece) and deeply subjective (editors like some things more than others).

This may have been these workshop writers' first exposure to this point of view, but if they intend to be professional writers it won't be their last, guaranteed. It could be that Wolfe wanted them to get an idea of what they'd be getting into for the next few decades of their lives. Those who couldn't hack Wolfe's getting into their faces about their writing might want to rethink their plans. In which case they might want to thank Wolfe for helping them bail out early.

Had I been in Wolfe's shoes, I would not have quit. I would have gone into that classroom and told them (those who would listen) that if they thought *he* was being rough, that they should just wait until their first batch of book reviews rolled in. The professional writing life is not for people who need to be affirmed. It's 98% rejection on a good day.

Writers also need to learn to stand their ground in the face of withering criticism. If your response to being slagged is to run away and write whiny letters about how your critic was unfair, *man*, are you ever in the wrong line of work. If you believe in your work, you fire back and you give as good as you get. You take your fight to your critic and make him or her back up the criticism. When your critics have a point, you learn and you move on. But when you think you're right, you argue it, tooth and nail, and you win or die trying.

Maybe Wolfe was trying to see if anyone in his group of writers would fight back. In her reportage, Ms. Lincoln prides herself on not losing her cool in the face of a barrage of criticism. I think she got it all wrong—I think she should have blasted back and made Wolfe explain his points. For all his experience, in the end he's just a man, not a burning bush. His word is not law. For all his experience, he *could* be full of crap. I can't speak for Wolfe, quite obviously, but if I unleashed a barrage of criticism and the response was a prissy, passive-aggressive letter of complaint, I could see how leaving might appear to be a viable option as well. I *wouldn't* leave—but I could see thinking about it.

Wolfe wrote: "Whatever rumor may say, the fault was entirely mine. It was my job to communicate with the students. I tried to, but I failed." He is bearing too much of the burden on his shoulders. Like my high school teacher, he taught his material in a way he knew worked, not in a way that was comfortable for his students. Students are not passive vessels; they have to meet their teachers halfway. It doesn't sound like these students made much of an effort. If this is their Odyssey, they're stuck eating lotuses, preferring a pleasant fiction to the harder road of writing—and defending their writing—in the real world.

AUTHORS WHINING

(March 22, 2004)

Since I seem to be writing about things writeresque the last couple of days, allow me to comment on Salon's lead story today, in which a book writer details how publishing has broken her heart, and has caused her to—brace yourself—get a day job.

Dear Author:

Aw, shut *up*.

Perhaps it's because my first exposure to the fiction market was a genre market (i.e., generally not a whole lot of money to throw around), or that my introduction to the book world was informational non-fiction (see above), or maybe it's because, I don't know, I think I would go *insane* if I put all my writing income eggs into one basket. But the point of fact is, **I never expect to support myself from writing books alone.** I just don't.

I love writing books, fiction and non-fiction both, and I want to do it the rest of my life. But given the amount I've made from my books so far—and I have sold six, so I figure I'm officially *not* a novice author anymore, even if it is still reasonably early in my career (I hope)—I'd be a fool to give up my various rather more regular writing gigs (i.e., my day jobs), which allow me a more consistent income. That income pays my mortgage and my bills and allows me *not* to freak out about what the hell I'm going to do if my next book doesn't sell to a publisher. If my next book doesn't sell to a publisher I still get to eat and have electricity. That's not bad.

The article also reveals the preciousness that some of the author clan seems to have regarding jobs not involving writing books. Clearly this writer sees a day job as the mark of failure, an idea that will come as a mildly offensive surprise to the thousands of authors who see themselves as successful and yet also manage to hold down a day job as well. Yes, maybe authors don't like the idea that they might need to hold down two jobs, but I don't have time for that sort of stupid thinking. My mother consistently held down two really crappy jobs for most of my childhood—one cleaning the houses of other people and the other varying depending on time and circumstance, but generally shitty regardless—and all she got out of it was a few bags of groceries at the end of the week and the knowledge she'd fed and clothed her kids once again. How *horrible* for writers that they might have to consider *lowering* themselves like that when all they get out of it is a published *book*.

Articles like this just enrage the hell out of me and make me think that my tribe is populated by jerks with a sense of entitlement the size of a hot air balloon (and as subject to the random winds). Are authors as a class this disconnected from the real world? My personal experience tells me no, but then again most of the writers I know are genre writers, who despite their fanciful subject matter seem to be grounded in the realities of the economics of writing books. I doubt this woman writes science fiction or romance.

Of course the article is also running in Salon, which has a history of chronicling the "misfortunes" of unfathomably privileged people who by all rights should be beaten in a public square for their heedless lack of clue. This article is right up that particular alley, a far-flung reminder that Salon's staff and contributor list of overfed liberal twits are still living in a 1999 mindset in which clever people are given stupid sums of money for no especially good reason, and are shocked beyond belief at the prospect of a world that is not, in fact, their personal teat, endlessly alternating between skim lattes and Diet Cokes.

I *do* feel sorry for this author, but not the way I'm supposed to. I'm mostly embarrassed for her that her *cri de coeur* comes off as the lament of someone who simply does not understand why the world does not love her and give her money and fame. I'm certain that this was not her intent; I do believe she's warning authors coming up not to make the mistakes she has in assuming that writing is still valued, and that the business of writing (that is to say, the publishing world itself) can still support the writer. To that end, I disagree with the first—people still love to read—and am neutral on the second. Yes, I would love for my book writing to support me and my family. I invite any of my publishers to make that happen. I assume it never will.

Paradoxically, this does not chain me down; I think it frees me to write what I want and not worry about anything other than the writing itself. To put it another way: Because I am not overly worried about money, I got to write a popular book on astronomy (now in its second printing. Yay!)—a life goal for me because I love astronomy and want to help other people love it as much as I do. I also got to write two novels pretty much exactly as I wanted to write them. They may be good or they may be bad (we'll see), but I didn't have to worry about anything other than writing books *I'd* want to read.

This is freedom as a writer. I don't know that I'd trade it.

COVER
LETTERS

(May 19, 2004)

Editor Teresa Nielsen Hayden has unsheathed her mighty Hammer of Editorial Whackination and is applying it liberally to one Todd James Pierce, a writer and English professor who has issued what TNH believes (and I for one concur) is some spectacularly bad advice on the topic of cover letters. Among the very bad advice: Lie about your writing credits, and be sure to accompany your submission with a phone call.

If you're a writer or would like to be one, I commend you to TNH's dissection of all that is truly stupid about this advice (her posting also has a link to the bad advice in question; it's at http://nielsenhayden.com/makinglight/archives/005212.html). The reason you should trust TNH on this and not Mr. Pierce is simple: TNH is one of the people cover letters get sent *to*. Her husband Patrick concurs that Pierce's advice is bad (with the immortal line: "This is stupid. I now have stupid all over me.") and as he's Senior Editor of Tor Books, that's *two* veteran front-line cover letter readers against one somewhat deluded cover letter writer.

TNH's evisceration is complete enough that I'll not replicate her efforts here, but I do want to call out the one piece of "advice" from Pierce that I think is well-near criminally wrong, excerpted below:

> *Tip Four: Still worried? Never published any-*
> *thing? Lie a little. Yes, lie. A cover letter is a persuasive*
> *document designed to do one thing: entice an editor or*
> *agent to read your manuscript. Say whatever you have*
> *to, within reason, to accomplish this.*

Uh, *no.*

First reason, as TNH notes: There's this thing. It's called Google. It allows an editor to fact-check your ass in 30 seconds or less. Now, it's understandable that Pierce may not have heard of it—this whole InterWeb thingy is new-fangled and all—but be assured that whatever editor you're attempting to scam *has.*

Second reason: It assumes editors are incompetent, which—surprise!—by and large they are not. If you don't think an editor knows all the major and most of the minor writing awards applicable to his or her genre, you're an idiot. Here's what's going to happen if I submit a manuscript to a science fiction house and note on my cover letter that I am the recipient of the prestigious William Booth Award for Science Fiction Writing, which doesn't exist. First, the editor is going to say, *I don't know this award.* Then there's the quick Googlefest to confirm the William Booth Award has been pulled out of my ass. And then there's the sound of my manuscript getting plonked, because why would an editor want to work with someone whose very first communication was full of *lies.*

Third reason: It's disrespectful. In this particular case, what you're saying to an editor is *you're stupid enough to fall for this,* and conversely *I'm clever enough to pull this off.* You're probably wrong, and if you're right, you won't be right forever. Read TNH's comment threads and you'll note that literary types and the people around them don't need much of an excuse to pull out their knives. Also, of course, and *apropos* to point number eight here, people *never* forget people who disrespect them. Lie to an editor, and for the rest of their life, any time your name pops up in their consciousness, it comes with a sticky note attached, one that says *Big Fat Liar*. Also, it's a small business. Word gets around.

As for the "make a phone call," let me tell you a story. When I was an editor, I specified no phone calls. So on the rare occasion that someone *did* call to follow up, what I would do is chat with them amiably and then when I was off the phone I would go and find their submission and stuff it into the SASE and send it back unread. Because they *failed*. **You must follow directions.** That's why they're *called* "directions." I had and most editors have hundreds of submissions from people who *have* followed directions. *All* of them deserve more consideration than someone who can't or won't.

Both of these examples of "advice" go to the heart of why much of Pierce's advice is rotten: it's not actual advice, it's a list of tricks designed to game the system—to cheat your way through. Well, as a writer, here's the thing to know about the editorial submission system: *It's not designed for you.* It's designed for the editors, to make *their* jobs easier. Is it fair? No, but so what? The editors are the gateways to money and publication. It's their ball, bat and field. They set the rules, and if you want to play, you have to play by their rules. It's simple.

Every attempt you make to game the system makes the editor's job harder. In the entire history of the world, no one has ever wanted to work with someone who makes their job harder. Sometimes they *will*, if the reward is substantial enough. But in the case of writing, you gotta remember: It's a buyer's market. Sure, you're brilliant. But there's a guy over here who is brilliant *and* who doesn't make the editor's job harder. Guess which one the editor is going to go with.

Here's how I would write a cover letter for a manuscript. Assume, please, that usual addresses and contact information are attached, and that I have done the research to know the name of the editor and the submission policy (which in this case we can assume has said to send the entire manuscript):

> *Dear [Editor's Name]:*
>
> *Hi there. I'm John Scalzi. Enclosed you'll find the manuscript for [name of book], a novel. It is approximately 98,000 words. I've also included a chapter synopsis.*
>
> *I'm a full-time writer and author of fiction and non-fiction books. My most recent novels are* Old Man's War *(Tor Books, 2005) and* The Android's Dream *(Tor, 2006).*
>
> *I've enclosed an SASE for your comments. Please feel free to recycle the manuscript.*
>
> *Best,*
>
> *John Scalzi*

And that's pretty much it. I'm a big believer that the cover letter exists to present minimal factual information that doesn't go out of its way to prejudice the reader concerning the actual manuscript. It says who I am, what I've sent, my relevant track record, and how to get hold of me. That's all it needs to do.

What if I didn't have previous publication? I imagine I'd say "this is my first novel" and be done with it. Lying won't do me any good (see above) and if it *does* turn out to be good enough to be published, wouldn't I be covered in the glory of hitting one out of the park the very first time? There's no shame in admitting you're starting out.

Don't lie. Don't be tricksy. And for God's sake don't make an editor's job harder. Be confident that your writing stands on its own merits. Ultimately, if you lie in your cover letter, what you're really saying is that what you've written isn't good enough to make it on its own. It's a bad message to send to editors. It's a bad message to send to yourself.

A LITTLE
LIBEL

(June 24, 2004)

I odd Pierce, the Clemson professor I wrote about last month, and who provided spectacularly bad advice to writers, has stuck his foot in it again, and in an interesting fashion. As a preface, know that Tor editor Teresa Nielsen Hayden savaged Pierce's "advice" on her personal site, particularly his advice to new writers to lie about their professional credits on cover letters (he's since amended it, but the unredacted version is available online in Google-cached form), and then in a separate entry wondered if Mr. Pierce had not taken his own advice with his professional credentials. TNH's crowd of enthusiastic admirers ran with the ball, making fun of Mr. Pierce all down the comment thread.

The thread lay dormant for a month or so until yesterday, when Mr. Pierce showed up, read the accumulated posts, was appalled that everyone was so *mean* to him and then promptly threatened TNH with a libel suit. What follows from there isn't pretty, mostly people (including myself) trying to explain to Mr. Pierce that people saying mean things about you does not actually equate to libel in the United States—it is famously tough to prove libel in the US, for reasons relating to that pesky First Amendment of ours—and suggesting to Mr. Pierce that if one does not wish to have one's publishing credentials openly questioned, perhaps one ought not be on record advising others to lie about *their* credentials. After all, when *I* give people writing advice, *I* tend to base it upon what has worked for me in the past, and I suspect most other writers do the same.

I believe we may have talked Mr. Pierce down from filing a libel suit, but given his comments in the thread, I still suspect Mr. Pierce isn't entirely clear why other people in the thread don't seem to support his position that he's the victim here. This is of course his own karma, and while in some respects I sympathize with the man—one suspects this is his first exposure to a comment thread pile-on, in which enthusiasts of a person's blog form a line behind the blogger to get their kicks in, and TNH's enthusiasts are both smarter and meaner than the average blogger's—in other respects I really don't sympathize at all. Fundamentally, he doesn't seem to get why working writers and editors are offended and appalled at the suggestion that one ought to lie about one's credentials to get work. And while I admit that it's probably more *satisfying* to posit the existence of a sinister cabal bent on destroying one's career than to actually examine the root cause of these folks' agitation (i.e., one's own really bad "advice" to writers), in the end Mr. Pierce would be better off doing the latter.

Also, from a purely rhetorical point of view, Mr. Pierce argues poorly: he makes easily refutable statements of some facts, does not seem in command of other facts (for example, he confuses slander with libel, which is not an encouraging thing when one is threatening a suit based on one or the other), and tries to use emotional appeals to support what he feels are facts (e.g., he feels that what TNH has done to him is wrong, therefore it should be clear that she has committed libel). He gets thrashed, and none too kindly. Again, it's easy to feel sorry for the guy. But then again, it's not like he's some 15-year-old comment board geek over his head in his first flame war; he is a professor of English at a major university. He *ought* to be able to argue clearly and for God's sake know the difference between slander and libel. Now, aside from Mr. Pierce's beatdown, he does bring up an interesting question: when *can* someone say he's been libeled? After all, Mr. Pierce does believe he's been libeled (or slandered, which apparently to his mind is the same thing). He hasn't been, but when could one say one is?

Bear in mind with what follows that I am not a lawyer. However, I have been a writer for newspapers and magazines for years, and as an editor I had to keep an eye out for potentially libelous material. In short, I have a reasonably good grip on what constitutes libel.

Now then: Let's say that one day I'm wondering around the Web, like you do, and I come across the following tidbit on someone's blog:

John Scalzi is a crack-smoking cat sodomizer. It's true. I've seen the pictures.

Naturally, I am outraged. How dare someone suggest I sodomize my cat while smoking crack! It's time to lawyer up! Or is it? There are questions to ask:

1. *Is* it true? I mean, if I actually *do* sodomize my cat and smoke crack, then I have no grounds to claim libel. I probably wouldn't want people to *know* about my feline-violating, drug-huffing predilections, because it will make for a lot of awkward conversational pauses at parties and would probably keep me from being confirmed by the Senate for any really interesting government posts. But if in fact I do those things, I have no recourse. But let's say that indeed, my urine runs clean and my cat runs without sexually-originated hip dysplasia. Next question:

2. Is my accuser aware that he's spreading untruths? If in fact I don't sodomize my cat or smoke crack, clearly there are no actual pictures of me doing either. If my accuser hasn't actually seen the pictures but says he has, we've cleared another hurdle for libel. On the other hand, if for some reason someone has gotten creative with Photoshop and ginned up fake pictures of me, my cat and a crack pipe, and then my accuser sees them and believes them to be real, then although he's *wrong* he probably hasn't committed libel (if he created the pictures and purports them to be real, then we're back into libel country).

3. Is my accuser's intent malicious? If my accuser is a member of PETA and has been shocked by the faked Photoshop pictures of me cornholing my cat, then one might reasonably argue that he's accused me out of genuine concern for the poor feline who is the object of my unwanted attentions. That's not libel. On the other hand, if the accuser hates my friggin' guts and wants nothing more than for me to die bastard die, then libel is back in business. Clearly, it would be good for me if the URL this accusation resides at is something like www.scalzisucks.com.

4. Have I been materially affected by the accusation? If someone says I'm an enthusiastic ravisher of animals, and yet my wife stays with me, my family and friends shrug it off and my employers chalk it up to the Web being the Web, then I don't have much of a case. But, if I was about to sign a contract on a book on cats, and the publisher rescinded the offer on the basis of the rumor I love cats too much, and a concern that the cats I don't penetrate I'll sell for drugs, then yes, I have a case. I also probably have a case if my wife leaves, my kid is picked up by Child Protective Services and all my friends stop returning my phone calls.

Note that for a really good libel case, *all* of these have to be in effect. And that's for *private* individuals—which is to say, normal people with normal lives. If for some reason I'm judged to be a public figure (say, due to my *extremely* low-bore celebrity via the Web and my published work), then I have fewer libel protections. Note also that if the information is expressed as opinion (i.e., "I believe John Scalzi sodomizes cats and smokes crack. I've heard rumors of photos that show this"), I'm out of luck. I'm also out of luck if the language used is "heated" ("Goddamn mother-fucking John Scalzi likes to poke his fucking cat with his tiny little meat and then shove a crack rock the size of a fuckin' rat into his crappy tinfoil pipe and suck on it like a Hoover on the overload setting") or if the work is satire ("Scalzi the Crack Smoking Cat Violator: A Musical Play in Three Acts").

And what do I get for it being so hard to prove I was wronged? Well, here in the US we have really excellent freedom to say what we want without worrying that opening our mouths to express an opinion will get us hauled into court—or into jail. Let's also note, by the way, that stricter libel laws don't actually mean that less libel happens; the United Kingdom has far stricter libel laws than the US but the UK press is just *vile* when it comes to rumors. Given a choice, I'll personally take a little less protection against libel for a little more protection of free speech.

For the record: I don't smoke crack and I don't violate my cat, and no pictures exist of me doing either. Although if someone whomps up something in Photoshop, be sure to send me a copy. I could use a laugh.

I, HOLLYWOOD

(July 20, 2004)

O ver on his journal, science fiction writer Bill Shunn has got himself worked up on principle over the *I, Robot* movie, which is based on the Isaac Asimov book of the same name roughly in the way a store-brand grape soda is based on an actual grape. Shunn is personally boycotting the film and thinks you should too, although with I, *Robot* pulling down a $52 million opening weekend, his boycott will have to play as a moral victory rather than an economic one.

I respect Shunn's position (and like him as a writer, which is always nice too), but am not the principled purist he is. I went and saw the film on friday, and I had quite a bit of fun with it; it was put together well (which means it moved quickly enough not to let one dwell on plot holes), it looked great, and it had just enough pathos in the form of the self-aware robot to be a bit smarter than the average loud summer film. In terms of Will Smith summer SF films, it was not as good as *Men in Black*, but better than *MIB II*, *Independence Day* and (shudder) *Wild Wild West*. Among director Alex Proyas' work, it's the least distinguished that I've seen (I haven't seen his *Garage Days*), but given the film is a hit, he's now got a chance to make more quirky films to re-establish his cred with the goth geeks. Overall, I give the film a "B-."

However, as a longtime professional observer of the film industry, I also went into the theater unburdened by the illusion that the film would have anything at *all* to do with Isaac Asimov's robot stories. This is a Hollywood motion picture, after all; nothing is sacred, least of all original texts, and least of all *this* particular case, since to my understanding the project initially started as an unrelated science fiction story about robots, onto which the *I, Robot* brand name was grafted as the rights to the property became available. In other words, this was a vaguely cynical exercise on the part of the filmmakers, at least as regards Asimov's work.

And, of course, this is SOP for Hollywood. Allow me to put on my pontificating hat here and tell you an obvious truth: **Hollywood doesn't care about source material.** When a major movie studio buys a novel (or in this case, a collection of stories) to adapt into a film, it stops being material of a fixed nature; it becomes suddenly fluid, and you'll find vast chunks of the book sliding out, getting rearranged or simply being ignored for the expediencies of the filmmakers and the studio. Let me make it even more clear: it is a rare book that makes it through the film adaptation process without great violence being done to it.

And this is not always a bad thing. I think some of the most successful literary-to-film transfers have been ones in which Hollywood does what Hollywood does—substantially guts and reworks the source material to adapt it to the needs of the filmmakers. The obvious example here is *Blade Runner*, which is of course a mightily reworked version of *Do Androids Dream of Electric Sheep?* by Philip K Dick. It's entirely possible a filmed version that is more faithful to the original novel could have been made; on the other hand, *Blade Runner* is excellent. It's a fair trade.

(This is not to suggest *I, Robot*, the film, is on par with *Blade Runner*. It's not; as divergent as *Blade Runner* is from *Electric Sheep*, it shares the book's primary narrative themes, whereas mostly what *I, Robot* shares with Asimov's work is robots, and the use of the Three Laws of Robotics as a plot device. But it *is* to say that in theory, and sometimes in practice, Hollywood's habit of gutting source material and reworking it is not *inherently* bad.)

Conversely, movies which follow their books to a greater or lesser degree (changing chunks here and there but still showing the recognizable plot lines of their literary progenitors) are not necessarily doing the books any favors: Hollywood appropriation of literary SF in this way often ends pretty badly, and the video stores are littered with the wreckage to prove it: *Dune. The Puppet Masters. Starship Troopers*, which I must confess I enjoy personally but which I know Heinlein fans throw their hands up in horror over (poor Heinlein has yet to have a good film made from his work). And let's not forget *Bicentennial Man*, as long as we're on the subject of Asimov. There are books which *do* make the transfer substantially unmolested—I think the adaptation of Carl Sagan's *Contact* is a good example—but they are rarer than not.

I readily grant that it's very likely a movie version that was more faithful to Asimov's ideas could have been made (Shunn directs folks to an unproduced screenplay, written by Harlan Ellison and Asimov himself), and possibly *should* be made. But it wasn't and hasn't, for whatever reasons. *C'est la Hollywood*. I'm not necessarily going to take it out on *this* version because of it, especially if this version has the imprimatur of the Asimov estate. And in any event, *I, Robot* the book remains in its unmolested state, and as of this writing is #40 on the Amazon.com sales list, a height

I doubt it, now over a half-century old, would have achieved without Hollywood's unsubtle violations. If a new generation of readers use this movie as an entry point to access Asimov the writer and other science fiction writers, well, speaking as a science fiction writer, I can live with that.

CELEBRITY
BOOKS

(January 12, 2005)

Now, as long as we're on the subject of writing, let me answer a question posed in one of the comment threads, which is:

> *As a writer, what is your perspective on the sensationalist books that are released and just absolutely bought up by the truckload by the general public? Case in point. The Amber Frey book that came out last week, where she's documenting her relationship with Scott Peterson. Anyone that doesn't know who that is, hasn't had a television on, read a newspaper, or visited a news web site in a VERY long time. Anyway, how does that make a published author feel? Someone who has worked years at their craft to get published and recognized, and yet this person is in it for "15 minutes" and gone. I realize publishers don't care about the content as much as the earning potential. I was just curious as to an author's perspective.*

As a writer, I'm almost entirely unconcerned about it. To begin with, most of the time the books folks like Amber Frey write (or more accurately, someone else writes so as not to make the putative "author" look like a total idiot) and the ones I write aren't really addressing the same audience; it seems really unlikely that there'd ever be a time when someone is in the bookstore agonizing over having to choose either *Old Man's War* or *Witness: For the Prosecution of Scott Peterson*. So I don't really gnash my teeth with each sale, thinking "that could have been *my* book." It wouldn't have been my book. Nora Roberts or John Grisham, on the other hand, might be annoyed—the whole melodrama of the Scott Petersen case is right up their respective textual alleys. But you know, they're not exactly hurting.

Secondly, life is capricious and weird, and there will always be someone who does not seem to deserve the fame and wealth thrown at them. Amber Frey's great claim to fame is being huckstered by Scott Peterson into having an affair. Is this a firm foundation upon which to build a lasting career in the public eye? No, but it'll *do*, and to be flatly honest about it, someone would have written up a lurid tell-all about Frey's relationship *anyway*, so why *shouldn't* she get the money for it? I mean, I'd rather she get the payday for her trouble than some hack spinning out the tale from newspaper clippings and court transcripts. Soon it'll all be over for Ms. Frey, and she'll go back to doing whatever it is she does when she's not known for being a murderer's moll. Hopefully, she'll manage her money well.

Ms. Frey's fortunes—or the fortunes of any person who suddenly erupts out of nowhere, makes a bundle of cash for dubious reasons, and then returns to obscurity as quickly as they arrived—affect me not in the least. The fact that she can get a book deal with a snap of her fingers while other people toil for years to do the same is monstrously unfair, but there are so many other things in the world that are monstrously unfair—and of genuine consequence—that this one example of unfairness is quaint by comparison. If other people want to be bothered by it, they should by all means worry that mental scab until their irritation is assuaged. But don't see why I would want to bother.

SYMPATHY FOR THE PUBLICIST

(June 6, 2005)

One piece of advice I like to give new authors (should they ask for advice) is that one should always, always be nice to one's publicist and do what one can to make the publicist's life easier. There are two reasons for this.

The first is that—*duh*—that person is promoting your book, and if you're a jerk to your publicist, that's going to affect the fervor with which they talk up your book to their various promotional targets. Since in addition to being a writer I am also a critic and exist on the other side of the publicist/artist equation, I know whereof I speak; the publicists I know will never *not* act professionally, but for all that you can *tell* who and what a publicist is excited about, and who and what they are not. This is subsumed under the whole "Don't be an ass" advice given elsewhere in the book.

The second is that the life of a publicist has remarkable moments of personal trial. I submit to you this bit of publicity sausage-making, from the floor of the BookExpo America in New York City:

On Friday afternoon, four young publicists from Tor Books were spotted in a corner trying to get one of them, Melissa Broder, into an 8-foot-tall hot-dog costume; it did have an air pump so the wearer could breathe. They were promoting "Invasion of the Road Weenies" (Starscape/Tor Books) by David Lubar.

Finally, they zipped Ms. Broder up. Fiona Lee took her hand, or paw, or whatever, and led her across the convention floor. "Would you like your photo taken with a giant weenie?" Ms. Lee asked, over and over again.

Would you like your photo taken with a giant weenie? Say it. Now. No, say it *out loud.* Now imagine saying it over and over and over again, to strangers and passersby, while you're holding the hand of a fellow publicist, who is dressed as a giant weenie. And that's your job. One does hope that David Lubar (who—as coincidence would have it—used to write humor articles for me when I was an editor, and good ones, too) appreciates everything these publicists were doing for him, and sends them flowers or something.

Now, as it happens, Fiona Lee is also *my* publicist at Tor, so I know from personal experience she rocks the publicity game in a magnificent way. And to her, I make the following solemn vow: My dear Fiona, at no point in our hopefully long and fruitful author/publicist relationship will you ever be required on my behalf to ask people to take pictures with a giant weenie, if for no *other* reason than I am a mere five feet, seven and some-odd inches tall, and am therefore an average-sized weenie at best. I also give massive props to Ms. Broder, who is not my publicist, but by God, being swaddled inside of a frankfurter would send *me* spiralling into a deep existential crisis, so I can only presume she is a better and mentally stronger person than I.

In any event, authors: Have sympathy for the publicist. It's not an easy job, in several critical senses of the word "easy." I'm not saying you need to *hug* your publicist or anything—depending on the author and/or publicist, this might be a bit much. But a nice "thanks for the work you do" is always in order. In that spirit: Thanks, Fiona. You're the best.

WRITERS ON WRITERS, AND IT'S NOT WHAT YOU THINK

(October 12, 2005)

Nor would you want it to be. Writers tend to be lumpy. Two of them together? Yeeeech.

Cherie Priest (who, for the record, does not appear to be inappropriately lumpy) notes an inherent wariness about meeting writers:

> *I tend to get along poorly with other writers until I know them well enough to know that they are not the sort of writers who piss me off. This may sound unfair and I'm sure that it is, but I automatically assume that other writers are assholes and that I don't want to meet them. The safest way to introduce me to other writers is to pretend that I'm a cat, being introduced to another cat in close quarters. Stand back. Get the water hose ready in case of emergency. Do not expect the introduction to go very well, and furthermore, be delighted if the encounter ends without blood loss.*

I find this amusing (aside from the fact it's amusingly written) because my experience is the opposite; by and large I find I get along just fine with other writers. But I also readily admit that I've spent almost no substantial time in the presence of writers who were not either *already* professional writers, or writing in a manner that subsumes individual neuroses underneath a need to get something in on a deadline (i.e., college newspaper stuff). Prior to selling a novel, none of the people I would deem as good friends were aspiring authors, and most of the people I know on a day-to-day basis aren't writers either. I've never been a workshopper or writer's circle type, so I never regularly crossed paths with other aspiring authors while I was one myself. The closest I came to any of this was the single fiction writing class I took when I was a freshman at the U of C, which served largely to establish that I'm not a "writing class" sort of person. Once I left college, I knew plenty of writers, but they were all journalists, which means (by and large) that they approach writing as a job, with daily performance expectations—i.e., deadlines and what have you.

In short, for the vast majority of my working life I've been isolated from the type of "writer" who sees writing as a holy calling, and have instead been exposed to the type of writer who sees it as their *job*, either as a journalist or as a working writer who relies on pay copy to pay the rent. These people—regardless of the type or style of writing they may engage in—tend to be fairly practical people when it comes to the "art" of writing; they talk shop the way mechanics talk shop, not the way theologians do (or are imagined to, anyway). Allowing for the general variation of human personalities (which is to say, some people are just assholes no matter *what* they do for living), I have to say that on average I've liked the working writers I've met.

Even if we don't share exactly the same worldview, we have a commonality of practical experience that gives us something to work with, at least until we all decide we're bored with talking about writing and go off from there.

I don't think I've met a working writer who does vomit on endlessly about the holy mission of writing and how it is an expression of their soul and so on, possibly because that sort of thing eventually takes a back seat to paying the electric bill, and possibly because if a writer is doing the "show don't tell" thing like they're *supposed* to do in the first place, they don't *need* to blather on about it; it's there in the writing, or should be. I don't know what I would do if someone was blathering on to me about the holy mission of writing, actually. I guess to amuse myself I'd picture them in their underwear, covered in blood-sucking leeches, turning powder blue as they slowly deoxygenate. Yes, yes. That is an image which will do quite nicely.

I think it also helps to meet the right writers, frankly. At my first science fiction convention, I knew not a damn person, so Patrick Nielsen Hayden basically appointed Cory Doctorow as my "con buddy" and Cory did me a mitzvah by introducing me to a bunch of swell folks who also happened to be writers, many of whom have since become good friends. These writers are simply good people—they're happy for their friends' success, they're generous in their friendship, and they tend also to be amusing as hell. Good role models for any budding writer. Next time you see me, have me introduce you to some of them. You'll like them. Or there's something wrong with *you*. Yeah, sorry about that.

WHAT PASSES
FOR AN ONLINE
LITERARY FEUD
THESE DAYS

(October 14, 2005)

An entry at the Galleycat Web site about my and
Cherie Priest's recent observations about writers (entitled
"Sci-Fi Writers Saner & Nicer, Probably Better Looking,"—
well, we're nicer, anyway), clued me in to the fact there's some
recent online literary-esque unpleasantness involving writers
Steve Almond and Mark Sarvas. The throughline here is that
Sarvas apparently bags on Almond's writing all the time in
his blog, and yet when the two of them were in the same
room at the same time during a recent LA literary gathering,
neither of them physically beat on the other, or even simply
immolated in some sort of bizarre literary matter/anti-matter
event that would have taken out the entire of Los Angeles'
literati, a tragedy from which it would have taken the US literary scene at least fifteen minutes to recover (Aw, shut
your hole. I'm from LA, damn you. I can make these jokes).

Almond wrote about the event, or lack thereof, in an
astonishingly awful piece that could only have run in that
miasmic hole of self-regard known as Salon; Sarvas batted
back in his literary blog. Of the two of them, Sarvas comes off

better, as he's internalized the blog world response of cool and bemused indifference to character assassination, including the delight in showing off some of the invective of the person attacking them. As I'm no stranger to such maneuvers myself, I appreciate the performance of the form. But neither comes off covered in glory. In this sort of thing, one rarely does.

However, the true bad actor here, if you ask me, is Salon. It actually *paid* Almond to write his unholy example of congratulatory literary fartsmelling. If the piece is genuinely indicative of Almond's personality, it's no wonder Sarvas didn't bother to seek him out, since he makes himself seem terribly unpleasant to be with or even near. Salon's editors should have taken Almond aside and said to him, "Now, you *know* this makes you look an ass, right?" Because if they didn't, they did the poor man a disservice. This is what editors are supposed to do: correct your grammar and keep you from making an ass of yourself in public (the two are not mutually exclusive).

But then Salon seems to make a business out of giving writers enough rope to hang themselves with. The seven most damaging words in the English language for the reputation of any novelist might very well be "I just wrote an article for Salon." If it weren't for the fact Salon's book section is serialing Cory Doctorow's latest novella, it would be almost entirely useless. Seriously, people: Salon's book section. It's *death*, in online magazine form. Enough said.

Authors, if you *must* write a piece in which you assassinate the character of some other writer, don't take money for it. That's just icky; there's something unspeakably unseemly about Almond having taken money for suggesting that some other writer might spooge in his pants just through the act of meeting him. It certainly doesn't make you want to handle any change that Almond might give you.

Really, now: do it on your *blog*. Unmediated, ill-advised gouts of ego-salving literary otherhating are what blogs are *for*. And then you get the fun of actually conducting a writer's feud in your comment thread, because the chances of the other writer *not* finding out you've written horrible things about them (via their daily egosurf through Google and Technorati) are slim approaching none. You get all of the dubious thrill of slapping down some other wordsmith, with none of the reputational taint of taking filthy lucre for what is essentially an exercise in degrading yourself.

Mind you, you shouldn't be initiating an online literary badmouthing in the first place. Other than cheap thrills, it doesn't do anybody any good, and you develop a reputation for being something of a twit (responding to a literary bad-mouthing is fine, although remember the key to success is *bemused indifference*, at least in the initial response. Wait to bring out the knives until the inevitable comment thread to follow). Better than debasing yourself online is to save that sort of thing for bar talk, where it can eventually settle into the sediment of literary gossip. It's more *fun* that way. In any event, I suspect it would lead to a higher chance of a physical altercation, which is what Almond seems to have been hoping for, anyway. Although, honestly, watching authors fistfight is like watching geese play Jeopardy. There's a lot of honking and squawking but no one ever gets to what they're supposed to be doing.

I don't know. Maybe it's just that no one knows how to conduct a real literary feud anymore, online or otherwise. It's a shame, that.

HOW NOT TO
PLAGIARIZE

(December 1, 2005)

I'm reading with interest a story about writer Brad Vice, who won a literary award and published a collection of short stories and then had the former revoked and the press run of the latter pulped when someone noticed that, hey, there's a short story here that seems at least partially written by another writer. Vice, who is a professor at Mississippi State University, said something along the lines of "whoops," claimed what he was really doing in lifting entire lines from another writer was an homage, and also claimed to be confused about that whole "fair use" thing. Meanwhile, industrious reporters have noticed the increasingly-aptly named Mr. Vice may have also lifted lines from other places as well, which certainly lends credence to the whole "shaky about fair use" thing, but also suggests the fellow may be a serial plagiarizer.

Now, an article from Media Bistro says to me that lifting junk from other writers is some sort of hot new academic trend—"Issues of intertextuality, embedded narratives, and literary borrowing and homage were very much in the critical air through the 1990s"—which I suppose marks yet another difference between academia and the real world, in that if I heavily excerpted text from, say, Olaf Stapledon, and presented it as original material in a novel, I suspect my editor Patrick Nielsen Hayden would bring down a big fat cudgel on my head long before I would have to make up some lame "It's an homage!" excuse and Tor became obliged to pulp an entire print run of a book. Out here in the wild, claims of wanton intertextuality gone amuck pale in the face of the economic cost of a major screwup.

(Also, come on, let's get real: homage is one thing and Plagiarism is another, and someone who makes his cash as a professor of English at a major state university damn well *ought* to know the difference—and know what's acceptable "fair use" to boot. If that's not actually in the job description for an English professor, it should be. And heck, Vice is the advisor to the MSU's English honor society! Oh, the shame. For its part MSU launched an investigation into Vice's lifting issues, which suggests tenure is not something he should hope for at this point.)

Being as I am someone who ripped off Robert Heinlein with wild abandon for *Old Man's War*, I'm the very last person who should suggest homage is not a legitimate literary technique. However, I would note that in my case I did two things which I think are of critical importance: One, I didn't actually cut and paste Heinlein's words into my manuscript, and two, I've been almost gaggingly upfront about what I've been doing. I thanked Heinlein in my acknowledgments, for God's sake. It beats deluding myself that no one would ever catch on to what I was doing.

As a matter of record, I did it again in *The Ghost Brigades*, where I found two ideas of fellow SF writers compelling enough to play off of them. One of the writers was Nick Sagan, whose ideas about consciousness transference in *Edenborn* were right in line with what I needed for TGB. Another was Scott Westerfeld; the brief space battle on pages 119-121 of TGB owes quite a bit to Scott's jaw-drop-pingly good extended space battle in *The Killing of Worlds* (his is the economy-sized version, while mine is the minuscule travel-sized version). In both cases I gave a head's up to the authors that I was going to play a riff off a theme they established, and of course I noted the riffs in the acknowledg-ments section of the book, listing the authors and the books, and describing them as "authors from whom I've consciously stolen."

Because why *wouldn't* I? I don't want to hide when I borrow; I'm comfortable enough with my own writing skills that I'm not threatened by acknowledging how much my writing is influenced by my able contemporaries. More to the point, I *want* people to know, because if they liked my tip of the hat, they should know where to find the inspirations. If reading *The Ghost Brigades'* acknowledgments (or indeed, this very bit of writing here) sends a few more readers to Nick and Scott, how could I not be happy about that? They're both excellent writers—I thieve only from the best—and deserve all the readers they can get. Also, and not insignificantly, it inoculates me from later accusations of idea poaching, since a guy who hands you an itemized list of the people he's borrowing from is clearly not worried about such accusations. I plead guilty, and hope you'll read these other excellent writers, too.

I'm not so sanguine about actual word theft, mind you; that space battle I mention above plays quite a bit like a miniature version of Scott's, but at least I typed all the words and word structurements out of my own brain rather than cracking open my copy of *Killing of Worlds* and transcribing from what lie therein. But I guess if one were going to do that, then one really should acknowledge it, shouldn't one? Because otherwise you end up with the situation Vice seems to be in. A little tip for you budding (and in Vice's case, not so budding) writers, which I encourage you to take freely and propagate widely: **Unacknowledged "homages" are often indistinguishable from plagiarism.** Yes, even when everyone "should" know the writer or the work you're homagifying (no, that's not a real word). A simple CYA statement at the end a story ("The author wishes to acknowledge [insert other writer here], whose story [insert story name here] this piece homagifies in an academically approved intertextual sort of way") will probably save a lot of heartache and print run pulping later.

It's a little early to expect homage or even simple theft of the books I wrote, but you know, if someone wants to play the changes on an idea I've had or a scene I wrote, groovy. Have fun with that. And if you want to note it in the acknowledgments of your book, even better. And if you want to send me a nice gift basket with an assortment of cheeses in it as a way of saying thank you, why, that would be best of all.

JANUARY IS LITERARY FRAUD MONTH!

(January 9, 2006)

I t looks like it's a shaping up to be a fine month for literary fraud, as two somewhat prominent authors are accused, in different ways, of not being who they say they are. The first is James Frey, whose millions-selling addiction memoir *A Million Little Pieces* may not be nearly   as   non-fictional as he's suggested, according to *The Smoking Gun*, which in a long investigative piece concludes that Frey either amped up or made up several of the events in his Oprah's Book Club-selected tome. The second is "JT Leroy," a young author whose tales of child prostitution and drug use were all fictional, which is good because it now appears the author may be entirely fictional as well, the creation of the couple who claim to have found him as a strung out-teen and helped whip him into literary shape. When Leroy makes public appearances, it's actually the sister of the male half of the couple. The author (if he exists) has issued a statement noting he uses stand-ins because of personal issues, but there are other things in the article to suggest he's vaporware.

I could not personally care less about whether JT Leroy turns out to be fictional or not. I find fictional people writing fiction no more or less objectionable than real people writing fiction, because it's *fiction*, after all. This looks to be a slightly more convoluted sort of ghostwriting thing than the people making the TV show *Lost* will be doing in the spring when they publish a novel "written" by "Gary Troupe," a passenger on that show's ill-fated plane (I believe he was the one that got sucked into the engine). Fake people writing fiction just adds another level of *meta* to the proceedings, if you ask me.

I understand some people who feel personally invested in the author will feel a bit betrayed to learn he doesn't exist. But you know, the nice thing is, the *books* still work, because they're fiction. I tend to be very results-oriented rather then process-oriented when it comes to fiction, which is to say what I care about is whether the book is interesting, not whether the author had to struggle up from drug addiction, or led a life of gilded ease, or was raised by ferrets or what-have-you. Maybe when I go back for my MFA (ha!) I'll care about the circumstances of the author and production of a book. In the meantime, really, as long as the book is good, I'm good.

I'm only barely more engaged with the James Frey fracas, possibly because I have a real antipathy toward the addiction memoir genre, which I find tiresome and self-pitying. Yes, it's nice former junkies have gotten both catharsis and a book deal. Doesn't mean I have to read the resulting book. Indeed, I have not read Frey's book; I feel pretty strongly that if you've read one "I'm a jackass junkie who abuses people, vomits on myself, gets hauled into rehab and comes out thankful I'm still respiring" tome, you get excused from the rest for all time, and I've read one, thank you very much.

(This should not be read as me saying I have no sympathy for people who were formerly addicted who have turned their lives around. I have friends and family who were and who have, and I'm *immensely* proud of them for having done so. I just hope they don't write a book about it. It's been *done*.)

Given my lack of interest in the book and antipathy for the genre, it's difficult to rouse myself into caring that the man defrauded millions of addiction voyeurs; indeed my first reaction reading the story was "well, he's sold three million. He's set anyway. Good for him." It's sort of the same lack of sympathy I'd feel for people watching "amateur" porn who might feel violated that the people making squishy noises there on their TV actually get paid to do it. Perhaps this makes me a bad person. I'm not sure, nor sure if I should care. I do know I'd rather watch amateur porn than read an addiction memoir, for what that's worth.

However, let's also keep focus on the fact that if *The Smoking Gun*'s article is indeed factually correct (and the site's been pretty good at being factually correct so far as I know), then Mr. Frey is a lying liar who lies, and his "memoir," whatever its literary qualities, is thereby a piece of crap. One of the things I find absolutely henious in the various discussions of this incident I've seen online is invariably there's someone who shows up and says something idiotic like the "literary" truth of the memoir is more important than the "literal" truth—i.e., it's okay to lie about events in a non-fiction book if it makes for a better story.

In a word: Bullshit. If one purports to write a non-fiction account of an event, one is, by definition, enjoined from writing fiction. If you write fiction and claim it is non-fiction, you are a lying liar who lies. Writing something that "feels" true does *not* make it true, and the fact that people will come forward to defend "truthiness" over truthfulness in non-fiction makes me want to go on a rampage with a shovel.

The tolerance for what one *wants* to be the truth at the expense of *genuine* truth is why we currently have a government which is of the opinion that truth looks exactly like a urinal.

If you're going to write fiction, call it fiction, for Christ's sake. People love *romans a clef* just as much as actual memoirs; indeed, they feel naughtier because you know the sex scenes are going to be better written. Writing non-fiction novels only works when you are Truman Capote, or intermittently if you're Tom Wolfe. I may be going out on a limb here, not having read him and all, but I'm guessing Mr. Frey is in fact neither of them.

~╫╫~ Chapter four: *~╫╫~*

SCIENCE FICTION,
OR,
DON'T SKIP
THIS CHAPTER,
YOU DAMNED
WRITING SNOBS

Yes, yes, yes. I know. Science fiction isn't real literature. That label gets reserved for the "literary fiction" genre, in which people hang about in their small towns and/or Brooklyn, collecting tiny experiential moments like coupons until they have enough to redeem for the Quiet Moment of Clarity just before the end of the story. Yeah, that's not a formula. But, hey, you know. You enjoy that. I'm happy for you.

Ah, I'm just messing with you. I read literary fiction like I read any other genre and I find it has more or less the same percentage of quality writers to hacks, good work to lame work, and memorable writing to forgettable tripe as any other genre. I don't particularly buy into the idea of one genre of writing being better than any other any more than I buy into the idea of one type of cuisine being better than

any other. Literary fiction is French cooking. Science fiction is Thai. Romance writing is all about chocolate. You can get good and crappy versions of each, and the snob who won't try some of each is merely missing out.

Be that as it may, to this point when I write fiction I write science fiction, because that's what I read most of for fun, and because that's what I like writing most of all. Science fiction and its conjoined twin fantasy comprise a genre that has its own set of concerns and controversies, both for its writers and its readers, and as I spend more time in the genre, I find myself commenting on these things more frequently. What you'll find here are some observations on some of the most recent trends in SF (that is "recent" as of late 2005 and early 2006) and some thoughts on where my chosen literary genre is going, or ought to go, in any event.

Why should you care if you don't write science fiction? Primarily because many of the concerns and controversies in science fiction have their analogues in other genres as well. Romance writers, say, are no less immune to the perception that their genre is all one type of thing than SF writers, when in fact both genres contain multitudes. Crime writers worry about reaching new audiences as much as the guys writing about aliens. Even aspiring literary fiction writers have as much to fear from publishing scams as the folks who imagine spaceships. The pieces in this chapter are tuned for science fiction writers, but the subjects under discussion here are universal.

As a side note, you'll note that two books get mentioned a lot in this chapter. One of them is *Old Man's War*, which makes sense because I wrote it. As with the rest of this book, many of my observations here are based on my own experience, and *Old Man's War* was the science fiction book I was pushing the most during the time most of these pieces were written. The other is *Accelerando* by Charles Stross, which came out in mid-2005. Charlie's book gets big play for two reasons: first, I think it's simply one of the best SF books of 2005 and should win lots of awards, and second, in many ways I find it a polar opposite of *Old Man's War*, for reasons that I detail in the entries you'll read in this chapter. So I bring it up quite a lot. I hope you'll take that as a hint that you should check it out.

That said, let's dive right in, shall we?

THE
CYNICAL WRITER

(October 18, 2005)

Pyr Books editorial director Lou Anders has some kind things to say about *Old Man's War* on his personal Web site, which is very nice of him. Anders' stewardship of Pyr has resulted in the imprint publishing some fine books, so for him to give OMW a thumbs-up makes me feel shiny and happy. He also says I'm a genuinely nice guy, and that my breath is fresh and minty! Okay, he didn't actually write the last part. Although I am chewing peppermint gum right now. I am entirely mintilated.

I note Anders' write-up for OMW, however, not for the praise but because he notes that he was initially not interested in the book:

> Not only is it "not the sort of thing I normally read," but initially, I quite deliberately held off checking it out. First, because I had heard that Scalzi admitted to (cynically?) seeking out what sells (military SF) and then writing same, and second because Scalzi put me off on his blog by quoting my most hated cliché, "If you want to send a message, use Western Union." I read for entertainment, yes, but part of what is entertaining to me is the act of learning, of bettering myself, and I have always held

the occupation of writer as something laudable on the level of that of teacher or scientist and expect writers to be somewhat smarter than average. I read to learn, and when a writer tells me upfront they have nothing deep to say, I take them at face value and go elsewhere.

Both of these objections make me smile, not in the least because they are objections absolutely based in fact: I did use the "Western Union" quote (although not at the Whatever, but in an interview for *Strange Horizons* magazine) and I did quite intentionally write a military SF novel after a trip to the bookstore to see what kind of SF was selling. It's all true! And with your indulgence, I'll chat a little about both.

Let's start with the "Western Union" comment, which is in response to this question:

> **DB:** *You note that Agent to the Stars was not a story "near and dear to [your] heart." Was* Old Man's War *that story, or do we get to look forward to another great story yet to come?*
>
> **JS:** *Well, to be clear, I like Agent's story very much — it was a lot of fun to think about and to write. But I think a lot of beginning writers try to write about something really important to them right out of the box, and to be successful in doing so, which I think is a little like expecting to hit a hole-in-one your first time at a golf tee. With my first novel (which, remember, I had no intention to sell), I just wanted to hit one on the fairway. So I chose a story about space aliens and Hollywood, which seemed to me a doable enterprise. And if I had mangled Agent beyond all recognition, it wouldn't have killed me or my desire to write.*

I'm a little wary about consciously trying to sit down to write a "great story." There's that old saying: "If you want to send a message, use Western Union." I want to write a good story, one that keeps a reader wanting to read. I think that within the confines of a good story one can write some fairly significant things, so long as they are in service to that story. In Old Man's War, I think I touch on a number of significant topics, but the operative word there is "touch." If you start calling attention to what you're doing, your story is likely to grind to a halt and you've pulled your reader out of the world you've created to go "Look! A significant point is being made!" I mean, it's better to assume your reader isn't stupid and can handle some subtlety.

In other words, the moment I say to someone, "I will now sit down to write My Great Story," I hope they will do me the courtesy of braining me with a shovel. For now, I'll stick to trying to write good stories, and see where that gets me.

I don't think Anders and I are in disagreement in terms of what writers can offer as entertainment and as entertainers. I'm certainly happy when writers offer more than mere plotting, and many of my favorite writers do. Entertainment doesn't have be vacuous, even when it is light. But as a *reader*, I live in fear of what I call the "John Galt Maneuver," in which a character stands in one place over an entire signature of pages, barfing up the author's political rhetoric like a bulimic Mary Sue. Science fiction's history is not exactly devoid of such blatant Galtery, which I think is to its detriment; as a writer of science fiction, I want to be more facile than that when and if I have a point to make.

Old Man's War is an interesting case for political/rhetorical messaging because its universe is so extreme: everyone is at war with nearly everyone else. Also, the political implications of this are only lightly touched on in OMW, in no small part because it's a "grunt's eye view" of that universe, and our hero has other things on his mind than social-political structure of the Colonial Union. His exposure to it is limited in any event, due to being a soldier and focusing on combat. But I think astute readers will have no doubt formulated some thoughts on what sort of government and society the Colonial Union actually is. In *The Ghost Brigades*, that story thread is explored rather more significantly, and should there be a third book, I think many of the consequences of what the Colonial Union is and how it is constructed will come to a head.

Certainly there is some authorial messaging going on in all this; I do have a point of view, after all, and anyway *someone* has to make decisions as to what's going on in this universe. It might as well be me, being that I am the author and all. But as noted, the goal is to have any messaging come through in the story, not in some character expounding at length (I *do* have characters expounding, mind you, both in *Old Man's War* and *The Ghost Brigades*. But I try to keep the expounding to a couple of paragraphs at most, and also try to let other characters get a word in edgewise). Also, as a writer, I want to make sure I put the story first, because that's what people have come to the book for. Any messaging has to fit the story, not the other way around. The OMW universe is a fictional and extreme sort of universe—any messaging has to play by the rules that the universe is constructed by.

(Indeed, that's one of the things that differentiates science fiction from "mainstream" fiction: Moral, political and philosophical choices are in the context of a created universe, not necessarily the one we live in. Some messaging won't map perfectly (or at all) into this universe, which (among other things) bugs people who don't want to have to stretch their smug little minds to accommodate a new set of rules— you can tell who these people are when they say things like "Science Fiction isn't real literature." Just smile, pity their tiny inflexible brains, and move on.)

One thing to point out (and which I suspect that Anders probably wouldn't take issue with) is that while enter- tainment can have a message, a message is not always required: sometimes something can just be kiss kiss bang bang (and in the case of science fiction, also rocket rocket). *The Android's Dream*, the book I keep mentioning but which almost none of you have seen—it'll be out late '06 from Tor—is, as far as I can tell, almost entirely message free. Indeed, the first chapter is just one extended fart joke, and believe me you, other than in an intestinal sense, there's nothing deep about that. Having said that, I think that chapter is one of the best things I've written—certainly one of the most *fun*, in any event.

Moving on to the "I wrote military SF because military SF was what I saw selling," I'll first note that Anders' reaction to this has not been unique: I know of several other people who were at least initially put off by this admission of mine, either because they've told me personally or because I've read it in their blogs (yes, I ego surf. This should not be news).

In a real sense I can sympathize. I think most people who experience art above the level of mere consumption want the art to be authentic, and to have that art created from a genuine place within the artist (bear in mind I'm using "art" and "artist" in very encompassing definitions of the words). You could very well argue that *Old Man's War* comes from a non-authentic place, creatively. I entirely admit I had no

real love for military SF prior to writing *Old Man's War*—
I didn't dislike or disdain it (which I think is important), it
just wasn't something that resonated with me in any significant way. I liked some books that could be classified as military SF but was neutral on or disliked others. If I had gone
into the bookstore that day and seen another subgenre of SF
taking up most of the shelf space, it's entirely possible (and
likely!) that I would have attempted a book in that subgenre
instead. For someone approaching my book, knowledge of
the novel's backstory of blatant calculation doesn't do
much for its credibility, or mine. Granted and noted.

But the book is what it is, and I am who I am. Hi, I'm
John Scalzi, and I write books to make money. I *also* write
books to enjoy myself and to amuse others. When the condi-
tions are right, these latter reasons take precedence over the
former—but I don't worry about it too much if it's the other
way around. What matters is whether what I write is any
damned good. I'm *very* concerned about that, for both business
and creative reasons. I want to write good books so readers
feel like the books have been worth their time and money,
and I want to write good books so that publishers feel like
they're going to do well by publishing me.

This is why I'm not in the least concerned about sharing
Old Man's War's publication history. Yes, I decided to write
military SF because it's what I saw selling, and as an unpublished fiction author, I wanted to maximize my chances
of selling a book and having it do well in the market.
Having made that decision, I wrote a story in that subgenre
that *I* would want to read, and generally speaking, I don't
appreciate reading crap. So there was the motivation to
write something that would sell, and also the motivation to
write something good to read. The former motivation can
reasonably be described as cynical, to the extent jumping

through any set of hoops can be defined as cynical; the latter motivation, I would argue, is genuine and authentic.

One of the great and interesting debates regarding art of any sort is to what extent *intent* is part of the evaulative process of the work—whether a work stands independent of its creator's motivation for creating, or whether it has to be considered in that context. I'm a creator, but for more than a decade before I was a creator I was a critic, and that time as a critic has made me wary of factoring in motivation when considering a work. More accurately, I think one can factor in motivation only *after* one has examined whether the work *works;* an artist may pour his heart and soul into a book or album or painting or whatever, but you know, if that book or album or painting sucks, it really doesn't matter if the intent was pure; it's still a bad book (or album, or painting or whatever). A really excellent work of art, on the other hand, may be enhanced by knowing the motivation behind it, but it has to be an excellent work of art on its own merits first.

Readers don't read process, they read finished books. Music listeners don't hear process, they hear the finished symphony. Moviegoers don't watch process, they watch the final cut of the film (until the director's cut DVD, anyway). *Process* is opaque and largely irrelevant; *results* are transparent and open to evaluation. Now, as it happens, people *do* often judge on process, if they know the process. But the funny thing about process is that it doesn't last—the work does. Sooner or later the work itself will stand alone.

I'm open about the process of writing *Old Man's War* because I think it's interesting (whether or not I think process is artistically relevant, I think it's fun to know about), and also because I'm comfortable with how the work came out. I think it's a good book, and it stands on its own in terms of being a good read. Will how the book came to be made affect how people see it? In some cases, sure; it already has. These things happen. But when it comes to cracking the cover and reading what's inside, people eventually deal with the book and the story. One hopes for a happy outcome when and if that happens.

SCIENCE FICTION OUTREACH

(December 15, 2005)

A question from the audience:

> *Greg Benford and Darrell Schweitzer have written an article on fantasy overshadowing science fiction and what that means to society.*
>
> *Rather than bias you with my opinion, I would like to hear yours since you're a rising SF writer of demonstrated intelligence. Hopefully, you'll blog about it. The article is at http://benford-rose.com/blog/?p=3*

I read it. For those of you that have not, the article largely consists of Benford glowering darkly about how the rise of fantasy is indicative of the rise of irrationality and an anti-science view in the United States, and Schweitzer appearing to do his best to talk Benford off the ledge.

Speaking specifically about Benford/Schweitzer, I think they're overthinking the matter by a considerable margin, because, of course, overthinking is what science fiction writers *do*. I think tying in the rise of fantasy and decline of science fiction to ominous cultural trends *feels* nice, because there's nothing like being held in the pitiless thrall of a world-historical hairpin turn toward entropy to make one feel better about the fact that it's JK Rowling making a billion dollars from her books and not you. *Let that woman have her blood money! We'll all be fighting the cockroaches for scraps soon enough!* However, I personally believe the problem is somewhat more prosaic, and it comes down to marketing and writing problems that science fiction literature has that fantasy does not; namely, that math is hard, and science fiction looks rather suspiciously like math.

Because science fiction literature *is* math, damn it. The best SF book of 2005, in my opinion, is Charlie Stross' *Accelerando*—more mind-busting ideas there per square inch than any other book this year, and on the off chance *Old Man's War* gets nominated for any awards this year, I shall be pleased to have my book lose to Charlie's. That being said, and as I've said before, *Accelerando* is for the faithful, not the uninitiated—and if you look at the significant SF books of the last several years, there aren't very many you *could* give to the uninitiated reader; they all pretty much implicitly or explicitly assume you've been keeping up with the genre, because the writers themselves have.

The SF literary community is like a boarding school; we're all up to our armpits in each other's business, literary and otherwise (and then there's the sodomy. But let's not go there). We know what everyone else is writing, and are loathe to step on the same ground. This means SF is always inventing new vocabularies of expression, which is good, but it also means the latest, hottest vocabularies are not ones that, say, my voraciously-reading but resolutely middle-of-the-road mother-in-law has any hope of understanding. It's math to her. Which is bad.

Meanwhile: Fantasy. *Jonathan Strange & Mr. Norrell*, by Susannah Clarke: my mother-in-law can read that just fine. Harry Potter? She's got the books. Neil Gaiman's *American Gods?* Maybe a tinge gothy for her, but she could handle it.

Just about the only commercially significant fantasy writer of the last decade whose books I couldn't give her right off the bat is China Mieville, mostly because Mieville is generating a fantasy mythology informed by the tropes of recent SF (his fantasy is like his remade characters—a delightfully grotesque mashup). I think of giving my mother-in-law *Perdido Street Station* and giggle for the rest of the night. But, as I said, Mieville's the exception, not the rule (and anyway, I love his writing enough for the both of us).

Fantasy writers are no less in each other's armpits than SF writers, to be sure, but they're not pushed to reinvent the wheel every single time they write a book; the vocabulary of their genre evolves more slowly. It's not math, or if it is, it's not math of the higher orders, and people like my mother-in-law can dive right in.

And this is the point: Fantasy literature has numerous open doors for the casual reader. How many does SF literature have? More importantly, how many is SF *perceived* to have? Any honest follower of the genre has to admit the answers are "few" and "even fewer than that," respectively. The most accessible SF we have *today* is stuff that was written decades ago by people who are now *dead*. You all know I love me that Robert Heinlein as much as anyone, but why does my local bookstore *still* have more of *his* books than anyone else's in the genre? The most effective modern "open doors" to SF are media tie-ins, which have their own set of problems: they're fenced-in grazing areas that don't encourage hopping into the larger SF universe, and also, no one *but* reconstituted geeks want to be seen on the subway with a *Star Wars* or *Star Trek* book in tow.

Thanks to numerous horrifying lunchroom experiences growing up, SF geeks are probably perfectly happy to be let alone with their genre and to let the mundanes read whatever appalling chick lit and/or *Da Vinci Code* clone they're slobbering over this week. (Now, there would be a literary mashup for the ages: *The Templars Wore Prada!* It'd sell millions!) But then we're back to the Benford/Schweitzer lament, aren't we: SF is getting lapped by fantasy in terms of sales and influence and will probably continue to do so. It's all very well to say the world has turned its back on SF, but if SF authors and publishers are saying this while resentfully suggesting that we didn't much like that stinky world *anyway*, and that it's much more fun here with all our friends, who, like, totally get us *already*—well, let's just say I find I lack much sympathy for the genre if this is going to be our position.

Darrell Schweitzer wrote in his lament that if someone wrote a SF novel as compelling as *Stranger in a Strange Land*, that people would read it *despite* it's being science fiction. I find this formulation incredibly off-key. People *are* writing books as compelling as *Stranger in a Strange Land* today; they're simply writing them for an audience who has *already* read *Stranger*. And God knows that any science fiction book that apologizes for being science fiction or that begs the reader to try it even though it's science fiction (horrors!) is doomed to failure, because no one follows up on a pity read. They won't call it tomorrow, they won't send an e-mail, they won't ping it when it's on IM, and they'll pretend not to see it at the next party they're both at. A pity read is an awkward, awkward thing indeed.

What we need are people who are unapologetically writing science fiction—and are unapologetically writing science fiction *for people who have never read science fiction before*. You want new people to read science fiction? You want SF books to matter to the masses? Then do some goddamned *outreach*, people. Write an intelligent, fascinating, moving piece of science fiction for the reader who has always thought science fiction was something that happened to *other* people.

Don't dumb it down—people can figure out when you're typing slow because you think they're moving their lips when they read. Just don't assume they've read any science fiction other than that one time they were made to read "Harrison Bergeron" in their junior year of high school. Make it fun, make it exciting, make it about people as much as ideas and give them a fulfilling reading experience that makes them realize that hey, this science fiction stuff really isn't so bad after all. And then beg beg *beg* your publisher to give it a cover that a normal 30-something human wouldn't die of embarrassment to be seen with in public. If we can do all *that,* then maybe, just maybe, science fiction as a literary genre would be back on its way to cultural relevance.

Not every science fiction author needs to do this—the idea of some of our more bleeding-edge folks trying to model a universe for skiffy virgins is one best left unexamined—but *somebody* should do it, and the rest of the SF writing crew should cut those brave volunteers some slack when they do. The person who reads intelligent but training-wheels-gentle SF today could be the one who is devouring *Accelerando* or other such advanced works tomorrow. That's good for us, good for them, good for the genre and good for the whole damn known universe.

And that's what I think about that.

REVENGE OF THE SCIENCE FICTION WRITERS!

(January 28, 2005)

Here's a quick rule of thumb: Don't annoy science fiction writers. These are people who destroy entire planets before lunch. Think of what they'll do to *you*.

Thus learned PublishAmerica recently. PublishAmerica is a somewhat controversial book publisher that many authors believe is a thinly-disguised "vanity publisher," and whose book deals take advantage of people who want to be "published" authors more than they want to read the fine print of a contract (PublishAmerica—and for that matter many authors published by the house—rather vehemently deny this charge).

A number of notable science fiction authors, including James MacDonald, have warned aspiring authors away from the house, which apparently didn't please PublishAmerica, which noted on one of its online sites that "As a rule of thumb, the quality bar for sci-fi and fantasy is a lot lower than for all other fiction…[Science fiction authors] have no clue about what it is to write real-life stories, and how to find them a home."

Well, naturally, MacDonald and others sensed a challenge, so what a group of them did was get together to intentionally write an utterly professionally unsaleable book ("Plot, characterization, theme: none of them are to be found... Grammar and spelling take a drubbing," they wrote in the Web site they created after the fact), and then submitted it to PublishAmerica to see if it met the publisher's quality standards.

And what do you know? It did—*Atlanta Nights,* as the book was called, was accepted.

Here's a sample of text:

> "I'm glad you could give me a ride," Bruce Lucent muttered, his pain-worn face reddened by the yellow sunlight. "What with my new car all smashed and all."
>
> His old friend, Isadore, shook his massive head at him. "We know how it must be to have a lot of money but no working car," he said, the harsh Macon County drawl of his voice softened by his years in Atlanta high society. "It's my pleasure to bring you back to your fancy apartment, and we're all so happy that y'all is still alive. Y'all could have been killed in that dreadful wreck." Isadore paused to put on the turn signal before making a safe turn across rush-hour traffic into the parking lot of Bruce Lucent's luxury apartment building. "Y'all'll gets a new car on Monday."
>
> "I don't know how I'll be able to drive it with my arm in a cast," Bruce Lucent shoots back. "It's lucky I wasn't killed outright like so many people are when they have horrid automobile wrecks."
>
> "Fortunately, fast and efficient Emergency Medical Services, based on a program founded by Lyndon Baines Johnson the 36th President of the United

States helped y'all survive an otherwise, deadly crash," Isadore chuckled. He nodded his head toward the towering apartment building, in the very shadow of Peachtree Avenue, where Bruce lived his luxurious life.

And that's one of the better passages. There are also two chapters with the same number, and two chapters with the same text (though, I understand, not the same two chapters as have the same numbers) and various other violations of common and grammatical sense. It's not for nothing that the authorial pseudonym for this book is "Travis Tea."

(No, I didn't contribute. But I kind of wish I had!)

Naturally, when the book was accepted, the science fiction writers couldn't help mentioning it on various Web sites, and when PublishAmerica found out it had been hoaxed, it quickly rescinded its offer. But by then it was too late—the SF authors, aside from placing the "novel" up for sale elsewhere as an example of PA's quality standards, have also issued a press release recounting the entire tale that went out on the newswires today.

Lessons from this story?

1. If you're an aspiring author considering PublishAmerica (or any other similar operation), make sure you do due diligence before you sign any contracts;

2. Don't make science fiction authors angry. You wouldn't like them when they're angry.

PUBLISHAMERICA DOUSES SELF IN KEROSENE, LIGHTS MATCH

(February 17, 2005)

What an ass:

In an exclusive interview with SCI FI Wire, the president of PublishAmerica defended his company against charges by a group of SF and fantasy writers that his company is a "vanity press," despite falling for a hoax perpetrated by the writers. The writers, in response to PublishAmerica's criticism of SF&F writers, concocted a deliberately bad bogus novel, Atlanta Nights, and submitted it for publication to test whether PublishAmerica would accept anything; after the hoax was revealed, PublishAmerica rescinded its offer of publication.

Speaking for the first time about the hoax, Larry Clopper, president of PublishAmerica, based in Frederick, Md., said his company knew about the hoax before it became public knowledge and withdrew its offer of publication at that time... Clopper said many mainstream publishers similarly do not read the entire manuscript before making an offer of publication. "The hoax failed," Clopper said. "It was a very amateur gag."

In fact, of course, the hoax succeeded brilliantly. Here's why:

1. Clopper's contention that publishers make offers on completely unknown first-time fiction authors before reading an entire manuscript is appallingly wrong; either Clopper knows this, and is lying through his teeth, or he doesn't know this, and he's a monumental incompetent. It is *true* that publishers of fiction will ask that initial submissions consist of, say, three chapters rather than an entire manuscript. But the point of that is that if they like the three chapters, they will ask for the *rest* of the manuscript. You know, to *read*. Then and only then will they take a chance on a completely unknown first-time fiction writer.

Why? Because—to repeat—you are *a completely unknown first-time fiction writer*. If you're Stephen King, they might be reasonably assured that you can carry off the whole manuscript, since you have a track record of doing such things in a profitable manner. However, you can bet that whoever bought *Carrie*, King's first novel, read the whole damned thing before making the offer.

2. Even if we lived in an alternate world in which "mainstream" publishers *did* make utterly unknown first time fiction authors publication offers based on a partial manuscript, the fact of the matter is no reputable publisher would make an offer on *Atlanta Nights*, because no matter what part of it you read, it's all *bad*. Trust me: Writers who are regularly published know what it takes *not* to be published, for the same reason that, say, Eddie Van Halen knows what sounds like crap coming from a guitar. It is well within a competent professional writer's skill set to write so poorly that no reputable publisher would touch the work.

Speaking as a former acquiring editor, I'm here to tell you that *Atlanta Nights* is awful from the very first page.

Any acquiring editor worth his or her paycheck would have thrown the manuscript in the trash, or at the very least stuffed it into a self-addressed, stamped envelope to send it back to the poor bastard who wrote it. It takes less than 300 words to know the thing is unpublishable; as they say in the industry, one does not have to eat an entire egg to know it is rotten.

What sort of editor reads such an awful book and says to him or herself: By God, *this* needs to be published? One of two people:

1. A monumental incompetent;

2. An editor whose acquisition criteria are based on something other than those of a "traditional" publisher— which is to say, the need to sell the book *en masse* to people who have no relationship to the manuscript's author.

I'd be willing to buy into the idea that PublishAmerica's acquisition editors are incompetent, but let's be charitable beyond all reason and assume they are not. Call it a professional courtesy. That leaves non-traditional acquisition criteria, and that's pretty clearly PublishAmerica's scheme. Anyone who looks at PublishAmerica's practices gets the idea that the publisher is not in the business of selling to a mass market; it's in the business of selling to the writer and to the writer's immediate friends and anyone the writer can convince to carry the book. And of course there's a phrase that fits those kinds of publishers: vanity publisher.

Assuming someone at PublishAmerica did actually read *Atlanta Nights*, what they thought to themselves was not "Damn, this is good," but "We're betting this guy has a lot of friends who will buy this out of pity." And so PublishAmerica made an offer. One can reasonably assume that PublishAmerica has done the same with many of its other authors. Not all, possibly. But many.

And naturally, this does all those poor authors a tremendous disservice. By implying that in the real publishing world, crap like *Atlanta Nights* is actually and genuinely publishable, PublishAmerica gives these authors a heart-breakingly low benchmark of presumed competence for publishability. Authors who assume that being published by PublishAmerica means they've hit actual publication standards for competent writing will be confused when future work, written to the same level of competence, gets rejected in the real world over and over and over again.

And of course, that's possibly part of PublishAmerica's plan as well: to create a stratum of authors whose *only* publishing option is to go through PublishAmerica because they're not competent to be published anywhere else. The company doesn't see them as authors; it sees them purely as a revenue stream, and it's content to keep them hobbled as writers to do it. And if that's the case, PublishAmerica isn't simply a vanity press, it's also unspeakably cruel.

The hoax worked because it exposed one of two things: either PublishAmerica is staffed by monumental incompetents, in which case you'd be daft to publish with them, or it's staffed by cynical, black-hearted bastards who purposely deceive and manipulate their authors, in which case you'd be daft to publish with them. The third option is that they're both monumentally incompetent *and* cynical, black-hearted bastards, in which case you'd be daft to publish with them and they should probably be taken out and beaten with the spines of their own books. For starters.

However you slice it, PublishAmerica is bad news. The only good news about the whole *Atlanta Nights* hoax is that no matter what PublishAmerica does, it makes itself look worse. To which the only thing to say is: Good.

THE POLITICS
OF SF

(January 16, 2005)

A question from the gallery:

As someone who not only enjoys Charles Stross's work, but who drools over intelligent SF in general (i.e., as someone who considers cutting-edge SF the equivalent of Ghirardelli chocolate), I'm very interested to learn more about the "real-world" political perspectives of the SF writers I admire. (FREX: China Mieville: pseudo-Marxist; LeGuin: pacifist Taoist; etc...)

I've noticed that the worldviews of many otherwise insightful SF authors—including Charles Stross—become strangely conspiratorial and dogmatic whenever they address current political realities. Are all contemporary SF writers dedicated Leftists? Or what?

Specifically relating to Charlie Stross, of course, the best person to answer that question would be Charlie himself. I will note that personally, I don't find him to be any more politically dogmatic than other people; Charlie's politics and mine diverge enough to be noticeable, and yet he doesn't shy away from my acquaintance based on my doctrinal impurities. He does have a point of view, which is perhaps best summed up in this quote: "I'm a fuzzy-headed warm-hearted liberal, and I think fuzzy-headed warm-hearted liberalism is an ideological stance that needs defending—if necessary, with a hob-nailed boot-kick to the bollocks of budding totalitarianism." I don't see that as dogmatic so much as aspirational. In any event, Charlie can speak for Charlie.

As for SF in general, I don't think anyone's taken a serious political survey of SF writers—because why would you—but anecdotally speaking it does seem to me that most SF writers I've met are of two political stripes: Lefties and Libbies. The lefty camp includes most SF writers who are not citizens of the US, which makes some sort of basic sense because the UK, Canada, Australia and New Zealand are rather more politically and socially "left" than the US. It does also include the general mass of US SF writers, who can be widely classified as a subset of the American intellectual class, which is generally left-leaning, although I would hesitate to say exclusively so. The libertarian camp of SF writers—the Heinleinites, as I like to call them in my brain—are as far as I can see a small but vocal minority. You recognize them the moment they open their mouths.

This is speaking very broadly and anecdotally, mind you; I can think of several successful SF writers who I see as generally conservative, either politically or socially. Orson Scott Card is famously socially conservative, a position that is to some degree rooted in his religious tradition. John Ringo seems fairly conservative; he's been known to write op-eds for the *New York Post*. Holly Lisle also seems to be of a politically conservative stripe to me, on the occasion I've seen her write about her politics. And of course as individuals most SF writers and editors have their political quirks and streaks. I doubt rather seriously that you'll meet an SF writer who is doctrinally straight ticket for whatever their general political stance is assumed to be. That's because SF writers, as a rule, tend to *think* about their political positions.

Knowing the politics of an author is interesting but usually irrelevant to their work, unless the writer is writing specifically about contemporary politics (which would be unusual for this genre). My personal political views, for example, are almost entirely irrelevant for *Old Man's War*; the story might give you a small sense of my thoughts on the use of military force, but then again it might not, since I've seen the book described both as "anti-war" and as an argument for the wisdom of having "boots on the ground." If you were to give the average person OMW and ask them to divine my political positions based on the text, I doubt you'd get all that far. Equally, I'm not sure having read *Perdido Street Station* that I would have pegged China Mieville as a socialist, because his personal politics are not glaringly obvious in the book, or at least, they weren't to me.

And what about, say, a book like Allen Steele's *Coyote?* In the book, the US has been replaced by a hard-right political entity, against which a small group of colonists rebel—and yet later in the book there's an even larger socialist state, and the colonists rebel against that too. What does any of this say about Steele's politics? Is he a lefty, a righty, or the sort of libbie that just wants to be left alone? Any, or none, or (my choice) it doesn't matter, since Steele is after all writing fiction.

Again, unless authors are explicitly addressing politics in their text, their personal politics and positions are trivia at best. Some will argue that personal politics do matter more than I've suggested, and I will argue that indeed, there are people for whom they will matter more than they do for me. And possibly in a different time and place, they might have mattered more, and might again. To switch art forms here, it *does* matter, for example, that Leni Riefenstahl's brilliant cinematic eye was used in the service of the Nazis. But the average writer who supported George Bush or John Kerry in the last US election does not, shall we say, sink to Riefenstalian depths. Here and now, most SF writers' personal politics—left, right, or off the axis entirely—are not integral to how their work should be approached.

WHO THE HELL CARES WHAT'S WRONG WITH AMERICAN SF?

(April 21, 2005)

Charlie Stross speculates, with only the tiniest hint of *schadenfreude*, as to why all the Hugo nominees for Best Novel this year are British—or, more accurately, why none of them are American. After politely offering the olive branch of coincidence, Charlie's off-the-cuff speculation is that American SF writers are depressed:

> *Here I'm going to shortcircuit the endless debate and bring up my proposition: that the shape of American SF, as with British SF, is determined by the cultural zeitgeist, by the society's own vision of its future. And I propose that the American future is currently uncertain, unpleasant, polarized, regimented, and pessimistic... This is not the place to list all the controversies or uncertainties haunting the American psyche in the wake of 9/11. Nor am I going to leave any hostages to fortune by prophesying either a reinvigoration of American hegemony, or a Soviet-style collapse. I'm agnostic on the matter. What I am willing to assert is that this uncertainty is haunting science fiction and warping the sort of fiction that is being written.*

This follows to some extent on a LiveJournal entry by Canadian James Nicholl, who asks: "So when exactly did the US stop being fertile soil for real SF?" and also suggests that American SF writers have a case of the doldrums, which shows up in depressing futures with restricted civil liberties.

I don't know. Personally speaking, I must have missed the memo to be depressed, since none of my SF (at least as it applies to earth) is pessimistic about the American future; indeed, on that far-distant day in which *The Android's Dream* is ever released you will discover that much to the consternation of other nations on the planet, it is a hale and healthy America that is the seat of the federal world government, and that sends representatives to the larger interstellar UN-like organization. I'm not incapable of writing darker-tinged fiction—I think you'll find that *The Ghost Brigades* is somewhat darker and more intense than *Old Man's War*—but neither do I find doom and gloom inherently interesting. It's a tool from the toolbox, and it has its uses, but it shouldn't necessarily be the first tool out of the box. And while I am not entirely pleased with the current American political/social scene, neither do I believe it portends the coming of the American Jerusalem and/or The Second Great Depression. The life of the US exists on multiple levels; some of the scarier levels are simply more obvious at the moment. We'll see where it goes from here. Suffice to say that in the long run, I am not unoptimistic.

American SF writers may indeed be trapped in a becalmed Sargasso Sea of the soul at the moment thanks to the various political and social shifts in this country. Alternately, it may be that the US writers are sucking up the tail end of a particular SF market trend that is rapidly playing itself out and American SF writers will now have to figure out where the hell to go to next. Or maybe they're all just in really crappy personal relationships. Maybe it's not the authors at all; maybe it's the *editors* who are buying stuff who are depressed as hell. As a reader, I find it difficult to actually *care* because I don't read by nationality, I read by author and/or story, and if the story is good, I simply could not give a squat where it is the author sits down to type his or her story.

As an author, I'm not totally disinterested in what other writers are doing—as I've noted before, I wrote *Old Man's War* because a trip to the bookstore told me that military fiction was what was selling, and as a first-time author, I wanted to sell—but I'm wary of making sweeping generalizations about what the lot of them are writing and how, or the contextual underpinnings of the work. The SF writing scene is small enough to have some uniformity in outlook, but people's lives and the ways those lives impact their work are intensely varied.

If American SF writers *are* uniformly depressed, well, I don't know, let's organize a field trip to someplace sunny for them. Let them frolic in the open air or whatever. Have them meet a nice person of their gender of sexual preference and then rut like stoats for a day or two. Call it charity. But if that doesn't snap them out of their doldrums, oh well. We've done what we can for them.

My theory as to why five Brits are Hugo nominees for best novel is pretty simple: leaving aside electoral noise like "hometown" bias and real or imagined personal relationships with the author, the five books nominated are just *really good books*. This is of course begging the question as to *why* they're so good, but just as American authors can have many reasons for slumping at the moment, these British authors can have myriad reasons for being at the top of their game, possibly some relating to nationality but other factors having little or nothing to do with it at all.

It's fun to ascribe an overarching reason for the inclusion of these five particular books, to try to impose some sort of uniform causality. But ultimately these rationales aren't going to pan out. Occam's Razor returns us to the "really good book" theory. It works for me.

The next piece you can see as a companion piece to "Science Fiction Outreach"—same ideas, many of the same examples, but a slightly different end point. —JS

THE MYTH OF THE SCIENCE FICTION MONOCULTURE

(August 2, 2005)

A number of people have written to alert me to Robert K.J. Killheffer's review of *Old Man's War* (among a number of other books) in the September 2005 issue of *Fantasy & Science Fiction*, with the intimation that the review is something of a slam. Well, of course, I love good slam, so I checked it out and was bitterly disappointed to discover it was a perfectly reasonable review; Killheffer gave points for style ("Scalzi's straightforward, muscular prose and tightly focused pacing yield an undeniable page-turner," which I imagine would be the money shot quote for Tor's marketing folks) but deducts points for substance or lack thereof ("but it amounts to little more than a fix for the Heinlein junkie"—not a money quote, although I'm sure an ambitious marketeer could make those last six words work with the judicious use of an exclamation mark).

That's fair. The only quibble I have with the review is the last sentence ("If *Old Man's War* is today's answer to *The Forever War*, it suggests a creeping superficiality in U.S. science fiction—the triumph of nostalgia and pastiche over fresh invention") and that on a technicality; OMW can't be an "answer" to *The Forever War* if for no other reason than I've never read that particular book. I keep meaning to—heck, I even *bought* it recently—but haven't. It's on my "to do" list, but I have a novel to bang through first.

In any event, inasmuch as I've cheerfully and frequently admitted ransacking Heinlein's bag of tricks for OMW, I can hardly complain when someone criticizes me for doing so. Live by the Bob, die by the Bob. And if you're sick of the Heinlein influence on science fiction, as Killheffer appears to be, it's perfectly reasonable to be underwhelmed by OMW. As for the book suggesting creeping superficiality, well. I would prefer it to be characterized as suggesting confidently sauntering superficiality, as sauntering is more fun than creeping (and easier on the knees). But what can you do.

Where Killheffer and I part company philosophically is in his overarching conceit for the review, in which Killheffer somewhat guiltily admits that US SF writers just aren't getting the job done for him anymore, so he's stepping out with the Brits, who seem to him to be as dangerous and exciting and forward-thinking as the US writers are conventional and backward-looking. This has been a topic of conversation here before, so I don't feel the need to revisit it in any depth, but what got me chewing the inside of my cheek in thoughtful irritation was Killheffer's summation paragraph, which reads:

> *SF, even more than other literary workspaces, cannot afford to get mired in nostalgia and ancestor worship. The sf of earlier periods should be treasured,*

*read and re-read for the pleasures and spirit only it
provides. But we cannot recreate it, and we should
not try, no matter how disappointing the develop-
ments of the past few decades might seem. It's time to
let Heinlein rest, and discover our own future. So
far it appears that U.K. writers come better prepared
to create twenty-first-century sf. But there's no
reason U.S. writers cannot do as much, if only
they'll turn their gazes from the past and look to
today—and tomorrow.*

Crap.

For two reasons:

1. Someone who likes the clean and breezy vigor of US-
bred contemporary SF but disfavors the pretentious over-
reaching twaddle of contemporary UK SF need only switch
the positions of "U.S." and "U.K" in that paragraph, and
then replace "Heinlein" with "New Wave," to have
achieved the equal and opposite (and, incidentally, equally
specious) conclusion.

2. It (quite possibly unintentionally) perpetuates the
myth of the science fiction monoculture, in which all science
fiction books are read by the same inclusive set of readers,
read in the same manner, and all the readers have the
same set of evaluative criteria. They're not, they aren't,
and they don't.

Now, once it's put out there in this way, the point seems
obvious. But since I see the SF monoculture worldview
pop-up over and over and over again, it must not be as
obvious as it should be, so let's go ahead and address it.

For our illustrative purposes, let's take *Old Man's War*
and Charlie Stross' *Accelerando*, which Killheffer quite rightly
gushes over in his review article, because it is, as the kids no

longer say, *teh r0xx0r*. Both of these books are undeniably
current and contemporary science fiction, and it's fair to say
that the two books have a fair amount of potential reader
overlap. They're both shakin' their booties on the science
fiction road. That being said, it's also abundantly clear that
while they're on the same road, they're also working different
sides of the street.

I take a back seat to no one in singing the praises of
Accelerando, which I think is just a tremendous science fiction
novel, full of the things that make you go *hmmm*, science
fictionally speaking. They might as well just announce
Charlie's Hugo nomination for it so the rest of us can go about
our lives. Having said that, if someone came up to me and said,
"I don't read much science fiction—heck, I don't read *any*—but
I think I ought to check it out. How about *this* one?" and then
held up *Accelerando* for me to see, I would probably suggest
against it, for the same reason I'd suggest against putting
a jet engine on a Big Wheel. *Accelerando* is high-octane geekery,
real inner-circle stuff, and you need to work up to it.

By the same token, if the guy who's homebrewed his
own flash memory-based multimedia player so he can enjoy
his Ogg Vorbis files—you know, the guy whose shirt has
the Linux penguin sodomizing Bill Gates—comes over and
asks me if *Old Man's War* has got the bleeding edge goods
he's looking for, the answer I've got to give is, well, no, almost
certainly not. *Accelerando's* and *Old Man's War's* audiences
overlap, but they are not the same.

Nor, I imagine, were the books written with the same
audience in mind. As I've noted before regarding *Old
Man's War*:

> The book is in fact intentionally written with
> non-science fiction readers in mind. Why? Well, it's
> simple: I want a whole lot of readers, and I don't want

> to give potential readers outside the sphere of SF the
> excuse of thinking the book is going to be inaccessible
> to them. Look, I'm not a snob. I'm in this for the mass
> market, and I want to nab readers who don't typically
> have science fiction as part of their reading diet.

And as it happens, that's where (anecdotally) a significant portion of OMW sales have gone—thanks to Instapundit and other non-SF bloggers who were enthusiastic about the book and recommended it, a large number of books got into the hands of people who read science fiction seldom or not at all. A large number of readers of my own sites were also not regular SF readers but bought the book because they were familiar with my writing online. When Tor and I offered up free e-books of OMW to soldiers in Iraq and Afghanistan, people bought the book because I was supporting the troops. I've got a few dozen e-mails from people who read the book that say "I don't usually read science fiction, but I read your book." Naturally, I encouraged them to start the SF habit.

I'll leave it to Charlie to note who he imagined his audience would be, but I suspect he would grant that *Accelerando* was written with already enthusiastic science fiction readers in mind, if for no other reason than much of the book was originally published as short stories in science fiction magazines, which implicitly address an enthusiast audience. This is not to suggest *Accelerando's* a cult item or has limited appeal—Charlie's made *Accelerando* a free download online, after all, which has gotten the book in front of ten of thousands (if not hundreds of thousands) of eyeballs, and the book's Amazon ranking is pretty sweet at the moment. Charlie naturally wants readers, and lots of them, and it looks like he's getting them. But I suspect Charlie knows the majority of those eyeballs are attached to SF geeks.

(NB: I could be wrong on this—Charlie may have in fact been writing for sf newbies and grandmothers. Ask him!)

I submit to you that *Accelerando* is well-nigh perfect; there's very little I would change about it (more lobsters. That's about it). It's also not for everyone, and not even for everyone who regularly reads science fiction. I think *Old Man's War* is fairly decent, too; it's also not for everyone, and not even for everyone who regularly reads science fiction. What both books do very strongly is engage their audiences, and give them a satisfying reading experience—and that is both healthy for the authors (hello!) and for the genre in general, since people who have been done well by science fiction will seek it out again. There's clearly room for both our books, since both have been published—in the same year, even!—and both appear to be selling briskly. Charlie's brand of science fiction isn't crowding out mine, or vice-versa. We live in harmony and love.

Science fiction emphatically doesn't need a monoculture, either in the literature or in the approach to that literature. There's no better way to kill it dead and to assure no one is left to mourn the ashes. What it needs—and what the range of titles noted just in Killheffer's article alone suggests it already *has*— is a multiculture that grows the audience for science fiction by giving that audience what it wants…whatever it is that it wants. Science fiction needs the US Heinlein revivalists and it needs the UK fearless futurists and it needs all the authors in the continuum between them, and those orthogonal to them as well. What you ask of all of these authors is simply that they write *good* books, the sort of books that make the readers go "Thank you! May I have another?" To which the answer is: "Yes! What would you like this time?" And then you *give* it to them.

That's how you create science fiction in the twenty-first century, and keep it rolling toward the twenty-second.

ASIMOV
AND THE CLETI

(March 1, 2005)

The Web site Boing Boing pointed to a cache of computer ads from the 1970s and 80s yesterday; one in particular caught my eye, of Isaac Asimov, sideburned and his nose all shiny, blandly extolling the virtues of the TRS-80 computer from Radio Shack against a dark, bare background. Why did it catch my eye? Here's why:

1. I have fond memories of being 12 years old and fiddling around with the TRS-80 Model III at the Glendora Public Library, writing little BASIC programs into the computer. I was quite the pre-teen BASIC programmer, which is to be understood as being the computer equivalent of saying "I was quite the architect with Lincoln Logs." From time to time I think about buying one off of eBay for nostalgia value, but since I already have a closet full of 80s electronic paraphernalia sitting there nostalgically, I doubt I can justify the purchase of yet another lump of 80s plastic. More's the pity.

2. If an art director today tried to get away with the sort of photo that's in this advertisement, his ass would be so fired. A background the color of bloody mud? The greasy shine on Asimov's face? Asimov's Captain Kangaroo-like suit? Fired, fired, *fired*. You wouldn't even use something like this for a local ad, much less one in a national advertisement campaign.

Our current culture has its ups and downs, but at the very least it's not as esthetically challenged as it was a quarter century ago.

3. Looking at the picture of Isaac Asimov, by the way, reminds me that I actually don't have a good idea of what his face looks like—The man for me was always characterized by his hair, glasses and goofy sideburns. Remove his lambchops in particular, and he looks just like any other schmoe. You have to think Asimov, not a stupid man by any stretch, was well aware that his distinctive look had at least *something* to do with his notoriety; because of it he's in the collective subconscious as the default image for "science fiction writer," not unlike the wild-haired Einstein is the default for "scientist." Now that I think of it, if you were to give ol' Albert a haircut and trim off his 'stache, I wouldn't have the slightest idea what *he'd* look like, either.

So a hint for all would-be science fiction writers: if you want to be known outside geek circles, work on some really distinctive hair, or, possibly, lack thereof. As it stands, at the moment I can't think of any truly distinctive-looking science fiction writers except for possibly Neil Gaiman, who's got an "I used to be the bassist for Echo and the Bunnymen" sort of look about him (shut up. It's a complement. Echo and the Bunnymen *rocked*), and then China Mieville, who's got that "Mr. Clean" look of his going on, and who in general is so far off the attractiveness bell curve for science fiction writers that I suspect the *actual* China Mieville is a troll-like guy in a dank room who sends this former competitive swimmer out to do his personal appearances, and feeds him dialogue through a cochlear implant. Admit it, "China"!! But yeah, aside from Gaiman and "China," there's not a science fiction author that you could recognize from ten yards out.

4. Aside the Asimov's lambchop issue, dwell on the fact that there's not a chance in hell that any major consumer-oriented corporation would even *think* to use a science fiction author to promote their wares these days, not even Radio Shack, who of late has been using Howie Long and Teri Hatcher to move their crap. We know they both can *read*, but other than that their literary talents are probably modest at best. Part of this has to do with now living in an esthetically-minded era (see points two and three above), but the other part of it is simply that there's no science fiction author who is currently such a part of the national conversation that he or she is seen as useful to push product.

Which is too bad. Not that I necessarily want to see, say, Cory Doctorow popping up to extoll the virtues of Snickers, or China Mieville with, well, Mr. Clean, although in each case the mind giggles like a schoolgirl to imagine such a thing. What I'm saying is that it would be nice if there *were* some science fiction writer who even the Cleti (plural of Cletus, *per* "Cletus the Slackjawed Yokel" from *The Simpsons*) knew of, even if they hadn't read his work. Because that would mean science fiction, as a literature, would actually have its hand in the national conversation, and aside the *Star Wars* media novels, it's not entirely apparent that we do.

It's not just science fiction, mind you. There are depressingly few scientists who rate in the national conversation, either: We've got Stephen "The Wheelchair Dude" Hawking, and then nothing. This is a change from even a quarter century ago, when you had Carl Sagan pinging the Cleti Awareness Radar. Now aside from Hawking, who's not even American, the closest thing we've got to a Cleti-pinging scientist is Bill Gates, and if he's a scientist, I'm a pony. (Steve Jobs isn't a scientist either, people. A real scientist wouldn't work himself into paroxysms of joy over flash memory.)

Now, this absence is somewhat related to the fact that there are now lots of people working overtime in the American culture to suggest that people who believe in evolution and the big bang also want to mandate forced downloads of child porn into your computer and give terrorists the key to your house. It's mildly worrying that scientists haven't found a way to counter this sort of thing. If they can send a man to the moon, they should be able to point out when someone is a complete fargin' idiot and have it stick. Something for the brainiacs to work on, in any event.

Asking that scientists and science fiction writers occupy a central role in American cultural life might be a little much to ask for, but I don't think it would be bad for at least one or two of them to be recognized on sight by the average Joe. It may require lambchop sideburns, but one of us should be willing to make the sacrifice. I suggest we draw straws.